GABRIELA VILHELMSSON

THE ART OF GARDENING

FOR INDOOR GARDENERS

SIMON VILHELMSSON

VAASA 2024

THE ART OF GARDENING
FOR INDOOR GARDENERS

I dedicate this book to my grandmother who inspired me to become a gardener. Thank you for all the Flamboyant seeds you saved for me.

Also, to my husband and editor, who crosses borders to make my dreams come true, literally.

© GABRIELA VILHELMSSON

FLOR DE CAFÉ PLANTAS - CNPJ: 37.940.783/0001-01

ISBN 978-952-94-9440-8 (PAPERBACK)
ISBN 978-952-94-9441-5 (EBOOK)

INDEX

PROLOGUE

The vast majority of people today are stuck in the same routine. From home to work, from work to home, where often the journey between these two places is more stressful than the day-to-day tasks themselves. There's no running away, that's life in big cities. I dare say that we are even used to such a routine. But then why, at the slightest sign of a holiday or vacation, our first thought is to escape the city, to the countryside or the beach?

The answer is simple: the lack of green. Our cities are gray, polluted and full of cars. To relax, we go to the mall on the weekend, or we hide inside the house. The truth is that our human essence needs direct contact with nature to maintain balance. A little sun, soaking your feet in the sea water or a walk in the park is enough to relax any tired mind.

For countries where the winter is rigorous and there are only a few months of summer every year, the importance of sunlight and nature is even more evident. At the smallest sign of summertime, my neighbours (in Scandinavia) occupy our backyard, exposing their skin to the not-so-warm northern summer.

Because of this, landscaping has changed over the years. It is not just the planning of large gardens, but bringing green closer to people. We've found that it doesn't take a lot of space to enjoy all the benefits of gardening. There are great chances that you have a potted plant at home, or even twenty pots (there's no going back at this point) and have already discovered how much the presence of green brings harmony into our homes.

However, indoor gardeners have one problem in common: lack of time. If you're reading this book, I'm sure you'd like to have green environments in your house or apartment, keeping your plants healthy and beautiful. At least, that's what I hear from my clients at my landscaping and gardening company in Brazil, Flor de Café.

THE ART OF GARDENING
FOR INDOOR GARDENERS

The bad news is that loving plants a lot isn't enough to keep them alive and thriving. After all, like any living being, they need basic care to survive. Always keep in mind that the plant you have at home is not in its natural habitat, that is, the climate, temperature, humidity and lighting conditions in your home are different from its place of origin. Therefore, it is up to the gardener (amateur or professional) to ensure that the vegetation adapts and finds the right conditions for its development.

The good news? It's easier than it looks.

In this book, I will introduce you to the world of amateur gardening, in an uncomplicated way, so that you can learn to take care of any plant and have the garden of your dreams, even for those who do not have the time or skills. Even if you live in a dark and cold country, who says you can't have beautiful tropical plants?

You'll find countless exercises, illustrations, and examples to help you become an expert in caring for your garden, no matter how big it is or where you live.

Gardening changed my life. I really hope that you, the reader, will enjoy this book and are able to realise how much nature and contact with green is one of the essential parts for a good quality of life.

GARDENING FOR EVERYONE

CHAPTER 1
GARDENING FOR EVERYONE

Do you need thousands of courses, college degrees, MBA:s, years of study and lots of money to be a gardener?

I'm not against studying. Quite the contrary, I studied a lot and I've worked as teacher.

But, I want to show you that gardening is for everyone. Even if you kill all your plants, if you've never studied, if you don't have money to invest, or if you don't have space.

Gardeners are all those who care about the environment, understand that plants bring well-being and harmony, and want to make the world greener.

LET'S TAKE A TEST?

		Question
☐	☐	DO YOU LIKE PLANTS?
☐	☐	DO YOU HAVE A WATERING ROUTINE?
☐	☐	HAVE YOU EVER KILLED ANY PLANT?
☐	☐	DO YOU ASK FRIENDS FOR A SPROUT OFF THEIR PLANTS?
☐	☐	DO YOU WORK WITH GARDENING?
☐	☐	DO YOU FERTILISE YOUR PLANTS?
☐	☐	DO PEOPLE ASK YOU FOR ADVICE ON PLANTS?
☐	☐	DO YOU FOLLOW PLANTS- AND GARDENING PROFILES ON THE INTERNET?
☐	☐	DO YOU RESEARCH ABOUT CHARACTERISTICS OF YOUR PLANTS?

If you answered ✓ for at least 1 question: Congratulations! You are a gardener.

WHAT DOES A GARDENER DO?

AMATEUR GARDENER

Amateur gardeners are everywhere — those who take care of their plants at home, take pictures and are filled with pride when a new flower appears.

They don't always know what to do (they may even have lost some plants) but they are always thinking about the next little plant they will buy.

PROFESSIONAL GARDENER

The main difference between a professional gardener and an amateur is that the former makes gardening a source of income.

Of course, when providing services, he will have to develop other skills, understand how plants work, the cycle of a garden and increasingly improve his knowledge in the area.

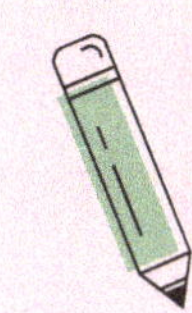

LADYBUG GARDENER

If you bought this book, you're already on your way to becoming a ladybug gardener. Ladybugs are the guardians of the garden. They have instincts that alert them to approaching predators and feed on the small pests that infest our plants. In different cultures, they bring luck and protection. It is associated with happiness and balance.

Whether you are an amateur or professional, a man or woman; if you love gardening and protecting your plants; if you always can be found surrounded be greenery in the garden — you are a ladybug. Green, nature and love for plants, are all already installed in your essence.

ACTIVITIES OF A GARDENER

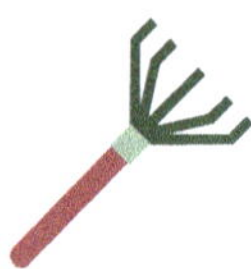

- Pest and fungi control.
- Pruning trees and smaller plants.
- Cultivation and planting.
- Grass cutting.
- Installation of irrigation systems.
- Identification of soil types.
- Soil correction.
- Use of different work tools.
- Garden cleaning.
- Advertising your work.
- Garden irrigation.
- Analysis of climate and environmental conditions.
- Implementation, creation and maintenance of gardens.
- Care for indoor and outdoor plants.
- Application of agricultural pesticides.
- Operation of gardening equipment and machines.
- Repotting and replanting plants.
- Visits to gardens, flower shops, orchards and suppliers.
- Conservation of large green areas.
- Creation of small arrangements, vases and planters.
- Plant identification.
- Tree planting and maintenance of public spaces.

WRITE THE 3 MOST IMPORTANT ITEMS	WRITE 3 SKILLS YOU ALREADY HAVE

WORKING WITH PLANTS – 1001 POSSIBILITIES

TERRARIUMS

They are trendy and can be a **great source of income**.
You can specialise in creating terrariums, using water techniques, miniatures and creating green worlds in glass.

SPECIALIST

You can be an expert gardener, focusing on just one plant species, or gardening technique – for example, become an orchid specialist. Have you ever thought about becoming an **authority** on the subject?

VEGETABLE GARDEN

There is nothing better, healthier and more rewarding than growing your own **food**. A gardener is able to grow vegetables, whether in large beds or in pots, creating amazing vegetable gardens.

GIFTS

Surely you've seen someone give out souvenirs with plants at weddings or other parties.
Terrariums, succulents, mini gardens. Use your gardening **creativity**!

SELLER

Gardeners can also be **employees** with a formal contract. Gardening- and flower shops are in great demand for employees who understand everything about plants.

ENTREPRENEUR

If you are a gardener with an inclination for business, have you thought about opening your own **company**? Commerce, service, consulting, etc. You can start being an individual micro entrepreneur or a freelancer and conquer the world!

ARRANGEMENTS AND VASES

The smallest of vases require skills and **knowledge**. A gardener knows all about layering, what plants to put together, and have a sense of space.

VERTICAL GARDENS

Gardens are not just on the ground. A gardener can create a vertical vegetable garden on the wall, a green shelf or a **porch**.

MAINTENANCE

Do you like hard work? Try taking care of a garden, farm or a condominium. Grass cutting, tree pruning, fertilising. But of course, you can also maintain **indoor spaces**.

GARDENS

There would be no gardeners without gardens! The gardener's challenge today is to create gardens in big cities, in small spaces and, often, on a tight **budget**.

COURSES

Who said gardeners are only good at taking care of plants? Have you ever thought about passing your **knowledge** on to others? You can give courses, consultations or even video lessons, like me.

PROJECTS

Want to be a **landscape** gardener? You can make and execute landscaping projects, taking your knowledge to another level.

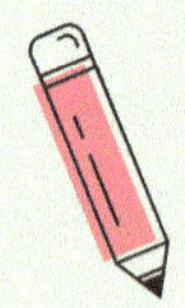

WHICH OF THESE ACTIVITIES ATTRACTS YOU THE MOST? IS THERE ANYTHING ELSE YOU'D LIKE TO DO?

GREEN FINGERS

CHAPTER 2
GREEN FINGERS

You have surely heard these phrases: "I don't have green fingers", "Plants don't like me", "I don't know how to take care of plants", "I have a rotten finger for plants".

Perhaps you have already said this. So I'll tell you the truth about gardening: There's nothing like **"green fingers"**. There are no people that plants get along with, who will never kill a single plant and who make everything grow and flourish.

Imagine two people who love plants. One has a beautiful garden, while the other is always killing their plants.

Which one has the potential to become a good gardener? Both! All the second person needs is **knowledge**. Knowledge of their plants' characteristics, natural habitat and what each one needs, individually.

There are no "green fingers", there are only people who do not give up on their plants.

FORGET THE
QUICK AND EASY FORMULAS!

Nobody can tell you how many times a week to water, when to fertilise or where to place your plant unless a study of your environment and routine has been done.

Each house, and each region, has different conditions of climate, temperature, ventilation, light, rainfall, etc.

The way I take care of my plants will be **different** from the way you should take care of yours. So, what now? In this chapter I will teach you my techniques.

NATURAL HABITAT

WHAT IS NATURAL HABITAT?

Have you ever seen an elephant walking through the streets of Paris? Or in the Amazon rainforest? Unless it escaped from the zoo, it's not common at all. This happens because the natural habitat of elephants is not France, nor a tropical climate.

Elephants are native to the African continent and some parts of Asia, where they inhabit large **savannahs and forests**. Compare the images below:

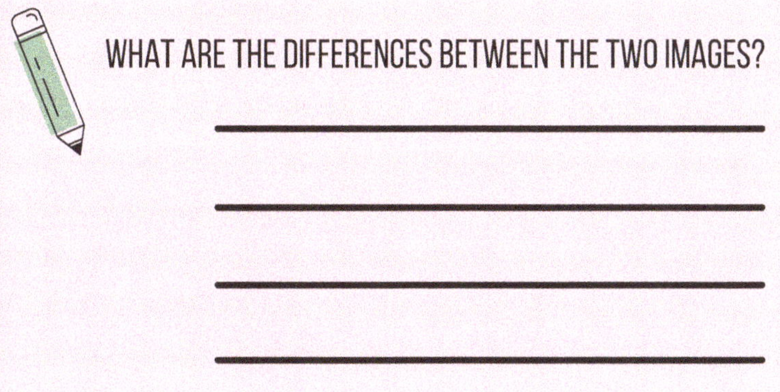

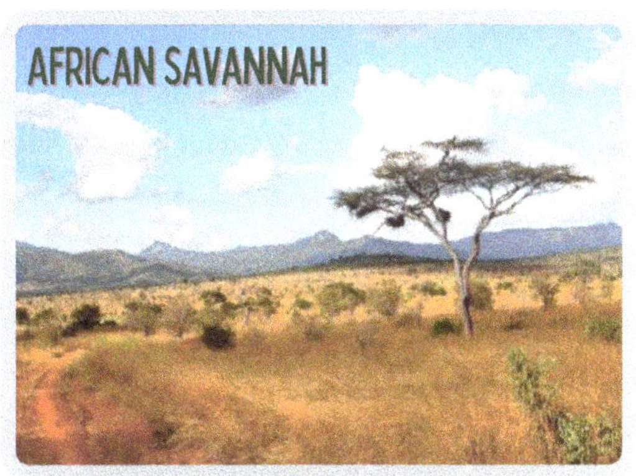

WHY DO I HAVE TO KNOW ABOUT ELEPHANTS?

You don't have to be a zoologist or a biologist to answer this question. Returning to the images on the previous page, were you able to identify the **differences** between rainforest and savannah?

We know that the elephant's natural habitat is the savannah. That's where it originated. We also know that in tropical countries — like Brazil, where I come from — there are different biomes and climates (you will learn about them in this chapter), but the **Tropical Forest** is typical of my country.

When analysing the images, you must have realised that the type of vegetation, temperature, insolation, air humidity, amount of water available, is completely different from one place to another. With all this information in mind, answer:

Can an elephant survive in a rainforest?

The answer is yes! Every species is able to adapt to new conditions. However, it will surely suffer from the **change of environment**. It will have difficulty finding food and water. There will also be different predators than it is used to, in addition to the sudden change in climate. It can take hundreds of years for a species to adapt to new territory, in the natural process of evolution. In short, don't try to bring an elephant to Sweden.

Have you noticed how zoos try to reproduce the same characteristics of their natural habitat? It's not just to make photos look good.

But you might still be wondering what elephants have to do with gardening. Finding the **natural habitat of a plant** is the first step to knowing how to take good care of them (and to stop killing them).

That's why landscapers are increasingly using only native plants in their designs to mitigate the effects of change. That doesn't mean we can't have a wonderful Flamboyant (Delonix regia) in the garden. If you know the origin of the plant you are working with, you already know the amount of water, light, humidity, ventilation, soil and conditions this species is adapted to. The gardener's **challenge** is to reproduce the conditions, wherever they are.

BIOMES

WHAT IS A BIOME AND WHY DO I NEED TO KNOW ABOUT IT?

A biome is a set of: a predominant climate, geological conditions (shape and characteristics of the soil), and a variety of unique fauna and flora — which survive under these specific conditions. In other words, it's a region with unique characteristics. A biome can also exist in more than one place. For example, Sweden and Canada share the same biome.

A **ladybug** gardener understands biomes and is capable of creating gardens anywhere in the world! Before studying gardening, let's learn about biomes. You will see how everything will be easier.

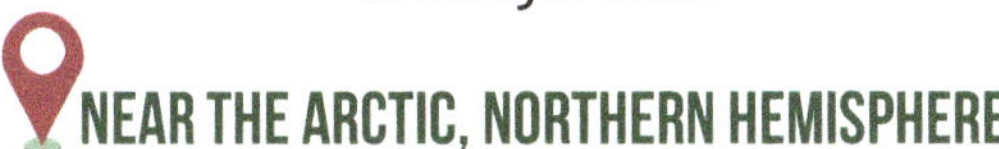

Mountainous region, covered by ice.
There is light, but no sun.
Few species survive, only a few
undergrowths.

NEAR THE ARCTIC, NORTHERN HEMISPHERE

Snowy region, characterised by pines,
cedars, bushes and herbs, with leaves in the
form of needles — as they do not lose water
in the winter and do not freeze.

NORTH AMERICA (CANADA), EUROPE AND ASIA

The 4 seasons of the year are well-defined
and the climate is cold as the altitudes are
higher.
Most plants are deciduous (lose their leaves
in the winter), such as oak.

CENTRAL EUROPE, EAST ASIA AND NORTH AMERICA, CHILE

Characterised by sun and rain, hot and
humid environment.
It has microclimates (the shade of the trees
creates a cooler environment).
It shelters a great diversity of species, of
different sizes.

AFRICA, ASIA, CENTRAL AND SOUTH AMERICA

MEADOW

Meadow, cerrado (exclusive to Brazil), savannahs, grasslands can be grouped in this biome.
There is heat but little rain, dry seasons and the soil is poor. There are spaced out trees with deep roots and undergrowth vegetation.

 **NORTH AND SOUTH OF BRAZIL, AFRICA,NORTH AMERICA**

CAATINGA

Little rain and not cold.
Deciduous vegetation, cacti and gnarled trees. The landscape turns green in winter when it rains.

 **EXCLUSIVELY BRAZILIAN BIOME (NORTHEAST)**

PANTANAL

Very hot region. There are many rivers, therefore, many floods.
This biome only exists in the Mato Grosso region (Brazil), due to the altitude and climate conditions.

 **MATO GROSSO - BRAZIL**

DESERT

Dry climate and high temperature.
It is cold at night, little rain and little vegetation. Plants in this biome have high water reserves.
The soil is poor in nutrients.

 **NORTH AFRICA, PART OF ASIA, USA AND MEXICO**

MANGROVE

It takes place where the river meets the sea.
The soil is clayey, the roots of the plants are aerial (for breathing).
There are many orchids and bromeliads.

 **COASTLINE OF TROPICAL REGIONS**

RESTINGA

It takes place on the beach.
It starts from the coast and goes towards the sea.
Undergrowth, trees, vines and bromeliads that grow in the sand.

 **COASTAL BEACH OF THE ATLANTIC FOREST**

AROUND THE WORLD

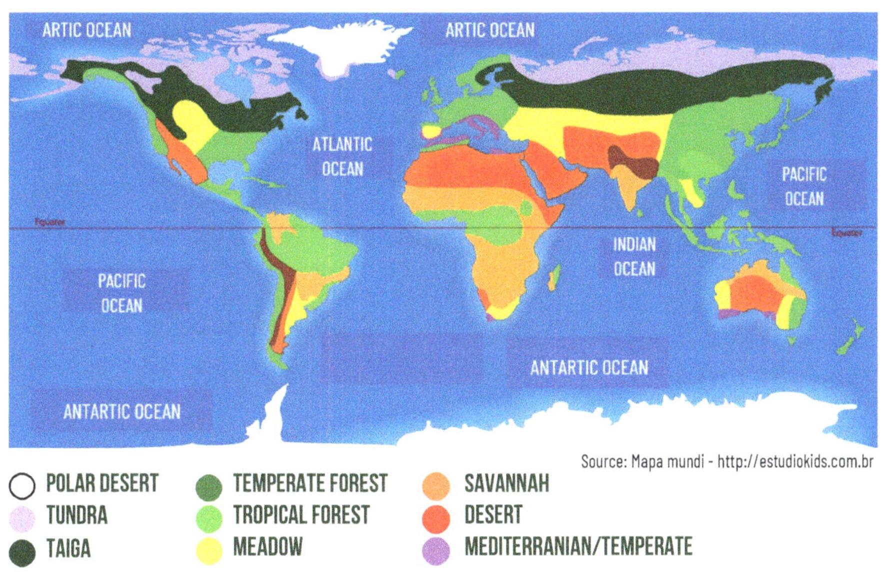

Source: Mapa mundi - http://estudiokids.com.br

In the map above, I highlighted the main biomes of the world. You can find others, and even more detailed maps (the meadow biome, for example, unfolds into several others) if you want to go deeper into the subject. But to get started in the world of gardening, these are the ones you need to know.

Note that in the northern hemisphere, above the equator line, the vegetation is adapted to colder climates, while the regions close to the equator and in the southern hemisphere, have the warmest climate. Keep this in mind when choosing species for your garden.

NORTHERN HEMISPHERE

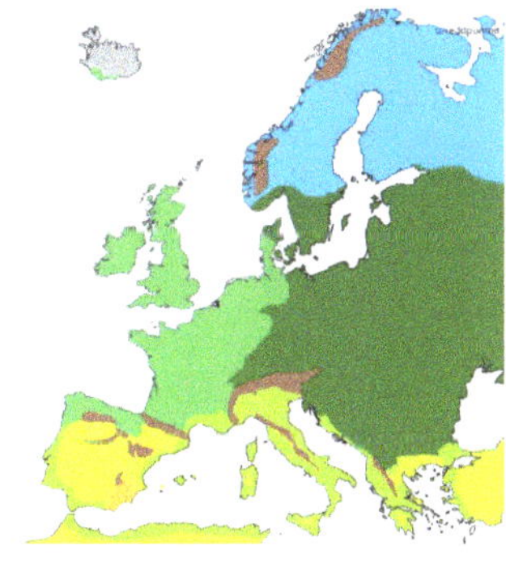

If you compare the North American- and European biomes it's easy to see how similar the biomes in the Northern hemisphere are. However, the distance between Europe and the equator line is longer, which means it would be harder to grow tropical vegetation, fruits and flowers there.

Because of the heavy winters in the northern-most regions, greenhouses must be used if you wish to grow tropical plants all year long. Whereas if you live in, for example, the U.S you could simply handle it by putting your plants indoors during winters.

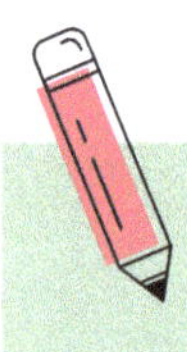

WHAT'S THE BIOME?

Look at the photos and describe their characteristics. What kind of weather? Vegetation?
From the information you highlighted, write which **biome** each image belongs to. Follow the example. The answers are on the next page.

Tundra

Cold weather, there's ice.
Shallow vegetation.
There is no sun, only light.
Mountains and frozen river. There are no trees.

CHECK YOUR ANSWERS

DESERT
TROPICAL FOREST
RESTINGA
CAATINGA
TEMPERATE FOREST
TAIGA
MANGROVE
TUNDRA
PANTANAL
MEADOW

LET`S PRACTICE!

Now that you know the different types of biomes in the world, it's time to understand how they interfere with **gardening**. Let's look at two plants: the fern and the cactus.

The fern's natural habitat is the **rainforest**. Remembering what we learned, the tropical forest has a hot and humid climate, with an enormous diversity of plants and animals.

Ferns are under the shade of large trees, where there is no sunlight, little ventilation. The soil is rich in nutrients, which come from available organic matter (fruits, leaves, animal remains).

Cacti, on the other hand, originate from arid climates, such as the desert and caatinga. In these environments, the soil is poor in nutrients and the climate is hot and dry. There is a high incidence of sunlight, so the plants have a larger reserve of water — to be used for long periods of drought, as rain is scarce.

THE IMPORTANCE OF KNOWING YOUR PLANT`S NATURAL HABITAT

Knowing this, it is easy to understand how to care for a fern in your home. Place your fern near a window where it gets light but not sunlight. Beware of excessive wind and dry weather. The soil must always be **moist and rich in nutrients**. Sprinkling water on your leaves is essential to maintain moisture. A strong sun and wind would dry the plant and burn it.

And the cacti? To keep them healthy, they must be exposed to the sun for most of the day and the **watering is spaced** — only when the soil is completely dry. They are very resistant, since they are species adapted to poor environments. No wonder they are known for being easy to care for.

Researching the natural habitat, country or biome of origin is the first step towards understanding how the plant works and widening your knowledge.

BE A PROFESSIONAL GARDENER

HALLWAY WITHOUT NATURAL SUNLIGHT

BACKYARD EXPOSED TO SUN AND RAIN

BATHROOM WITH A WINDOW

BALCONY WITH PLENTY OF NATURAL SUNLIGHT AND NO RAIN

I need your gardening services to decorate the spaces in the photos. To make it easier, I'll give you a list of plants and their natural habitats. Observe the environments to the side, considering their lighting, ventilation, amount of rain and sun, etc.

WHICH PLANT WOULD YOU CHOOSE TO DECORATE EACH PLACE?

See how you don't need "green fingers" to take care of your plants? Just don't go putting an Agave in a humid dark bathroom and **you will do fine**!

There is no absolute right answer to this exercise, but keep in mind that the more different the space from the natural habitat, the more likely the species will suffer and not develop properly.

THE 3 COMMANDMENTS

CHAPTER 3
THE 3 COMMANDMENTS

That you are a gardener, or want to be one, I already know. As such, I would like to welcome you to the **ladybugs' club** — where only those who love plants, seek to understand more about them, and are always improving their knowledge are accepted.

It doesn't matter if you are an amateur or a professional, if you want to take care of your plants or your client's — you know that contact with nature brings countless **benefits**.

SHALL WE TAKE A LOOK AT THE CLUB?

THIS CHAPTER WILL ILLUMINATE YOUR IDEAS ABOUT GARDENING!

Of course, this is a fictional club. But still, let's register and find out what kind of gardener you are?

1 I USUALLY BUY NEW PLANTS…

- A | When my plants die
- B | In the spring
- C | If I want a new one
- D | If I see one I like on Instagram
- E | To collect different species
- F | Every week

2 I WATER MY PLANTS…

- A | When my plants are dying
- B | I let the rain do its job
- C | Once in a while
- D | With a sprinkler
- E | 2x a week
- F | When I notice the soil is dry

3 IF I HAVE A FREE SPACE AT HOME…

- A | I cement it
- B | I grow a new lawn
- C | I put some plants in it
- D | I hire a landscape designer
- E | I buy a lot new vases and plants
- F | I search what would be a good plant for it

4 AT MY HOUSE…

- A | The gardener takes care of my plants
- B | I always buy flowers to decorate
- C | I have some plants I got on my birthday
- D | I have an auto-irrigated vegetable garden
- E | I have several different species
- F | I have an organic compost maker

5 I TAKE CARE OF MY GARDEN…

- A | If I have time
- B | In the spring
- C | When I remember to do it
- D | When my calendar reminds me
- E | Everyday
- F | Daily, if I see that they are in need of care

6 GARDENING FOR ME…

- A | Is extremely difficult
- B | Makes my home more beautiful
- C | Is cool
- D | Is trending
- E | Improves my life quality
- F | Is essential for life

WHICH CATEGORY DID YOU GET MORE POINTS IN?

THE OBLIVIOUS GARDENER

You only remember to take care of your plants after they have already died out of thirst. You think plants don't like you, find gardening too difficult, and end up giving up on your garden and paving it all over.

THE TRIBE-CHEIF GARDENER

Loves a rain dance. You depend on the weather to take care of your plants. Wait for the rain to water your garden and only tidy everything up in the spring.

THE WHATEVER GARDENER

You have some plants at home and you even like them. Water your plants with a glass, when there's time and it's all good.

THE XXI-CENTURY GARDENER

You don't have time to waste. You use sprinklers or automated irrigation system to keep your lawn green and your plants healthy. You are always up to date with news on social networks and applications to make your gardening life easier.

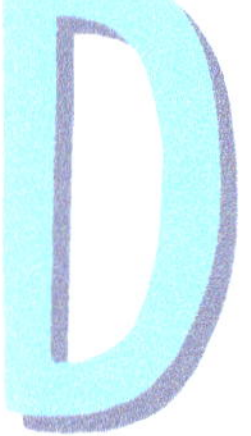

THE URBAN JUNGLE GARDENER

You live in the city, but your house looks like a jungle. You grow several different species and are always looking for a new one. You take good care of the garden.

THE LADYBUG GARDENER

Congratulations! You are an eco-friendly person who takes gardening seriously. You set aside time to take care of your plants, keeping them healthy and beautiful all year round. You cultivate native plants, have your own vegetable garden and are concerned with using only organic products. You are ready to work with gardening.

🌿 THE BENEFITS OF GARDENING

- It's a form of therapy.
- It improves mood and helps avoid depression.
- Helps with body health, either through food or the use of medicinal plants.
- It is relaxing.

- It is a sustainable practice.
- It makes the environment more beautiful.
- Creates more pleasant microclimates.
- Connects us with our origin.

- Improves sleep quality.
- Source of vitamin D - put on your cap and go take care of your garden.
- An inexpensive hobby that becomes a lucrative source of income.
- It connects you to nature.

- Regulates the humidity of environments.
- It's a great way to educate children.
- Teaches about the values of life.
- It develops the senses of contemplation, meditation and attention.

- Contact with the earth produces serotonin, the happiness hormone.
- Brings out a good mood, lightness and high spirits.
- Attracts beneficial animals for the balance of the ecosystem.

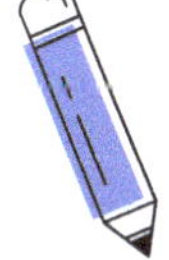

- Stimulates strength, dexterity and self-esteem.
- Prevents diseases and hypertension.

TELL ME, WHAT ARE THE BENEFITS OF GARDENING FOR YOU?

THE 3 COMMANDMENTS ⚖️

Now that you're part of the club and you know all the benefits of gardening, it's time to discover the commandments of gardeners. You need to know that there are 3 fundamental things for a plant, no matter where it comes from, its natural habitat, where it is, its size or species.

WATER

The first thing your plants cannot lack is **irrigation**. Water is responsible for chemical processes, absorption of nutrients by the root, photosynthesis (transformation of light into energy) and plant nutrition.

Seeds also need water to germinate. The cells of a plant only multiply in the presence of water.

FERTILE SOIL

Fertile soil means that the soil is full of nutrients. When taking a plant out of its natural habitat, the gardener must give it all the **nutrients** it needs to live. If any nutrients are missing, your plant will show signs.

LIGHT

You have already seen that light is responsible for **photosynthesis**. Plants feed in a different way than us animals. They need energy produced by photosynthesis. For a plant, no light equals no food.

Even if a plant is resistant to shade, it needs **light incidence**. It may be far from the sun's rays, but light must reach it.

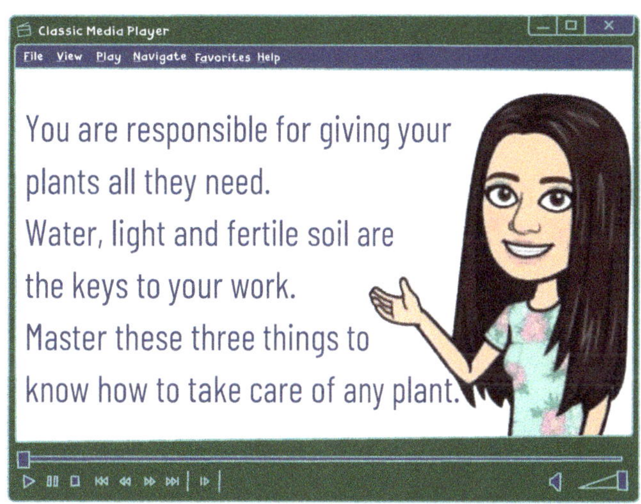

WHAT IS PHOTOSYNTHESIS ANYWAY?

Understand this essential process in plants, with the simple scheme below.

The leaves absorb the light.

Light is responsible for splitting hydrogen- and oxygen atoms in water molecules. H_2O is the formula for water. Remember that leaves stores water.

Oxygen is used to burn this sugar to produce the plant's energy, and then it is discharged back as steam. That's photosynthesis.

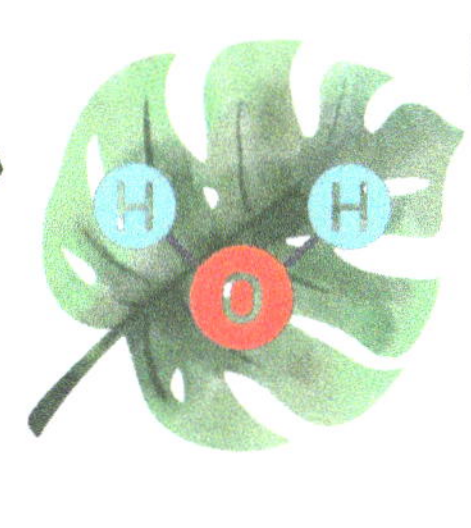

The hydrogen joins the carbon dioxide (CO_2) present in the air, turning it into sugar. The leaf also stores air.

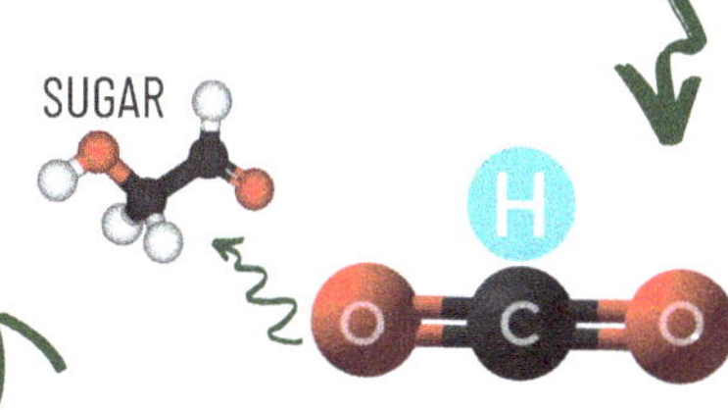

FREQUENTLY ASKED QUESTIONS  

What does a plant need the most 

Every plant essentially need 3 things: Lighting, irrigation and fertilisation.

When should I water my plants

Whenever the soil is dry. Put your finger to check if the substrate is dry. If yes, you should water it. If it's still damp, in most cases, wait.

Do plants photosynthesise at night 

No, photosynthesis depends on light. During the night, plants do their breathing process and release the gases they don't need.

Should I fertilise my plants 

Yes! A plant that is not in its natural habitat needs to be fertilised correctly, so that it can replenish its nutrients.

Do I need to prune my plants

At least, prune your plants after flowering. Also do periodic pruning of old, dry leaves and for light entry.

Does every plant need sunlight

There are plants that don't require sunlight. They are called half-shade plants. But, understand that every plant needs light.

POST A PICTURE OF YOUR PLANTS AND TAG @GARDENING.TAIGA ON SOCIAL MEDIA!

PLANT OBSERVATION

CHAPTER 4
PLANT OBSERVATION

In the previous chapter you learned that lighting, irrigation, and fertilisation are essential for plant growth and development. But what happens when the amounts of light, water and fertiliser are inadequate? Usually, the first signs that something is not going well will be quickly noticed in the leaves, stems and flowers. Let's learn to identify these signs!

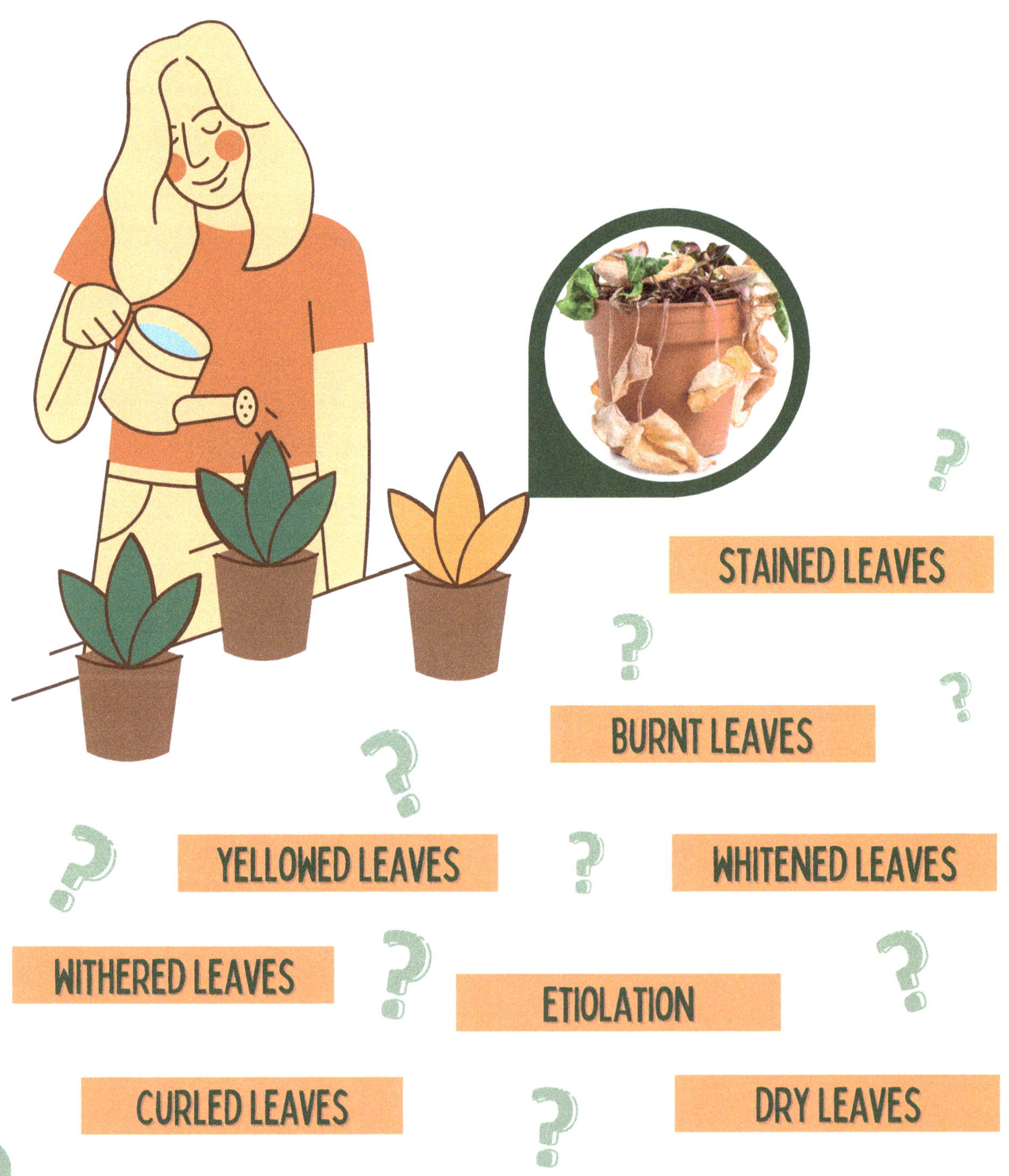

WITHERED LEAVES

Withered leaves are a sign of **lack of water**. First the roots try to absorb all the water present in the soil. Once this is dry, the plant begins to absorb all available water reserves in order to survive. Starting from the tips of its leaves, it takes all the water to the centre of the plant, sucking its strength and starts withering.

Comparing with the human body, where the first signs of dehydration are dry cuticles, hair and skin. It is a natural reaction of living beings, concentrating their scarce water reserves for survival.

WHAT TO DO?

Emergency watering. Place your plant in a basin and let the roots absorb as much water as they need.

WITHERED LEAVES

WITHERED LEAVES

Withered leaves are a sign of **overwatering** too. What do we do now!? It's easy to identify the cause. Place your finger on the substrate and see if it is moist and compact. If so, it's a sign of overwatering.

In this case, the plant tries to breathe and absorb air through the roots. Excess water makes the earth compact and without oxygen, making this process rather difficult.

WHAT TO DO?

Stop watering for a while. Only water when you are sure the substrate is completely dry.

Make sure the drainage layer is adequate and there is no water pooling at the bottom of the pot. In more severe cases, replant in a dry substrate.

BURNT LEAVES

Leaves with burnt ends can be a sign of many things. It is not possible to identify the cause without first analysing the entire plant and the environment in which it is located.

Some causes of burnt ends are: lack of humidity, too much wind, air conditioning, excessive watering, fungi, inadequate fertilisation, lack of light, too much sun or a too small pot.

Do you see how it takes a complete analysis to get to the real problem? **Perceive the environment** and eliminate not possible causes. Identify the problem so you can treat it correctly.

WHAT TO DO?

Change the plant's location, adjust watering, lighting and fertilisation, apply fungicides, replant, prune burned ends.

CURLED LEAVES

Soft, yellowed and curled leaves are a signs that the plant is lacking fertiliser.

Remember when the last time you fertilised your plants was? As a professional gardener, I know that most people with plant problems say that the fertiliser is up to date. Between us, we know this is not true.

Incorrect fertilisation is the biggest cause of diseases in the plants we have at home.

WHAT TO DO?

Adequate and organic fertilisation — including plants that are **out of your sight and reach**. You know that vase you forgot in the bathroom?

BURNT LEAVES

Completely burned leaves, as if they had been hit in layers, are a sign of fungi.

A fungal disease called Anthracnose makes the leaves get a **burnt appearance**, which can easily be confused with sunburn, incorrect fertilisation, etc.

For this, it is again necessary to carry out an analysis of your plant: it is in the shade, you always fertilise, maintain humidity and water correctly — probably the burns are a symptom of fungi. Fungi are present throughout the plant. Not just on some leaves.

WHAT TO DO?

Correct the causes of fungi and pests: incorrect irrigation, lighting and fertilisation. Apply **fungicides**.

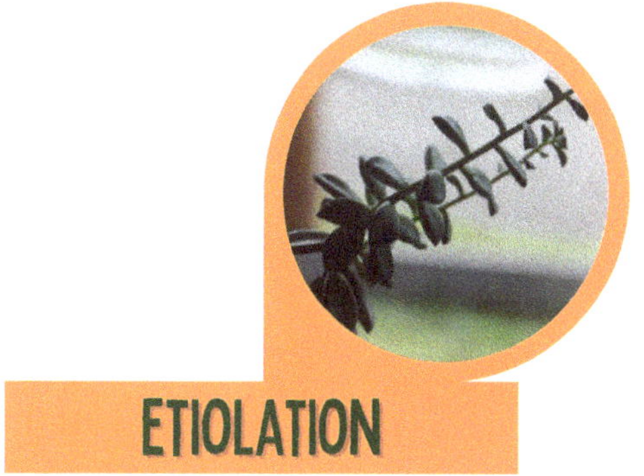

ETIOLATION

The great evil of plants that stay indoors. When you notice that the stem abnormally **stretches** towards the light, growing so fast that leaves are not born, becoming small and spaced, this is a sign of insufficient lighting. In addition, the leaves can turn a pale green, almost white colour.

If you notice the leaves have turned white, almost like a **dust layer**, chances are your plant has been infested by another fungal disease, Oidium. Lack of sunlight and vegetation is the perfect combination for this fungi infestation.

WHAT TO DO?

Give light to your plants, gardener! That doesn't mean they need to roast under the sun. But correct lighting is the key to the development of your plants. Remember photosynthesis? Bring your plants closer to the window, place them at a **suitable height**.

DEAD PLANTS

This is a very common problem among gardeners and is (often) caused by **over-fertilising**. Few people know how to fertilise correctly, no matter if it is chemical, mineral or organic fertiliser.

Excess fertilisation makes it difficult for the plant to absorb nutrients and water. The plant withers and its tips are burned. Growth is also exaggerated, sprouts- and weak new leaves begin to be born, being exposed to pests. Eventually, it dries up and dies.

Read and re-read the chapter on fertilisation, so you don't run that risk.

WHAT TO DO?

Strictly follow the information on the packaging and do not overdo it.

IF I HAVE A SICK PLANT, WHAT SHOULD I DO FIRST?

CHECK ✓ ONLY WHAT YOU THINK IS ESSENTIAL.

- [ ] Fertilise the plant
- [ ] Check if the lighting is adequate
- [ ] Emergency watering
- [ ] Look at the leaves to identify spots
- [ ] Apply fungicide or pesticide
- [ ] Remember the last time you fertilised
- [ ] Check the soil for moisture
- [ ] Spray water on the plants
- [ ] Observe the environment where it is
- [ ] Get it out of the sun

If you checked ✓ any **ACTION** items, before **identifying** the cause, remember that you should not fertilise, water or relocate without knowing if this is what the plant needs.

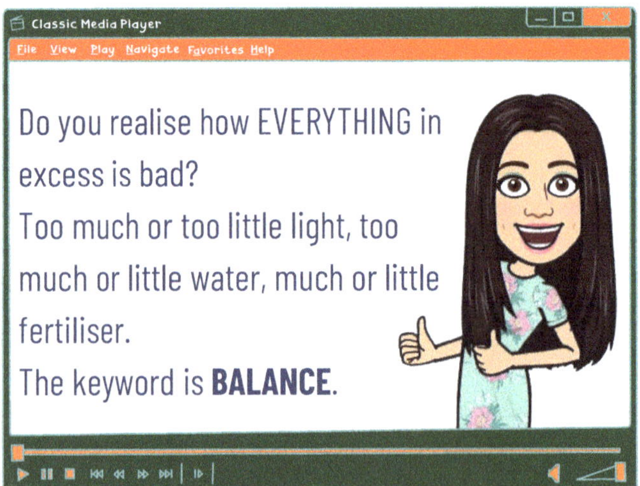

GARDENER'S SECRET TIPS

CHAPTER 5
GARDENER'S SECRET TIPS

There are some things you only discover through practice and **trial and error**. I learned a lot during my career as a gardener and landscape designer — in the courses I took, in my experience taking care of plants, since I was a little girl.

In this chapter, I'm going to share some amazing tips to make your gardening life easier. Those "golden tips" that nobody tells. Things I only tell my ladybug students.

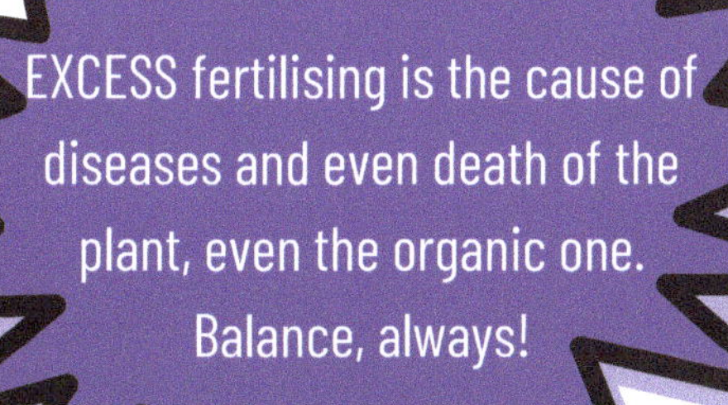

EXCESS fertilising is the cause of diseases and even death of the plant, even the organic one. Balance, always!

Get in the habit of saving organic matter to fertilise your plants.
Peels of vegetables, fruits, egg shells, leftover tea and coffee, dried leaves, etc.
How about mixing it with soil and making a mini composter at home? Never spend money on fertiliser again.

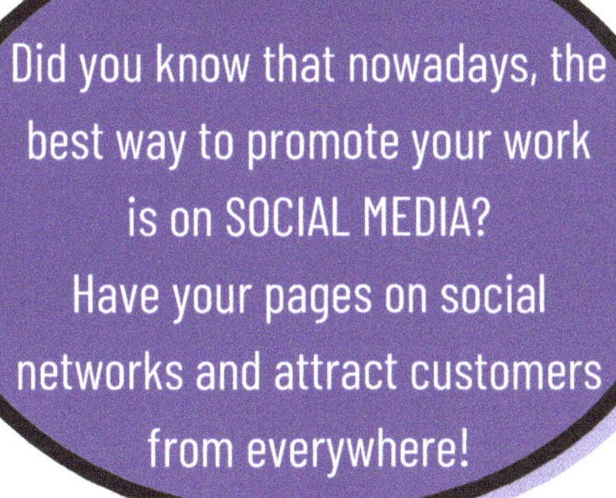

Did you know that nowadays, the best way to promote your work is on SOCIAL MEDIA?
Have your pages on social networks and attract customers from everywhere!

You know the FIRST thing a professional gardener cares about?
Safety at work.
Wear gloves, goggles, cap, boots and sunscreen!

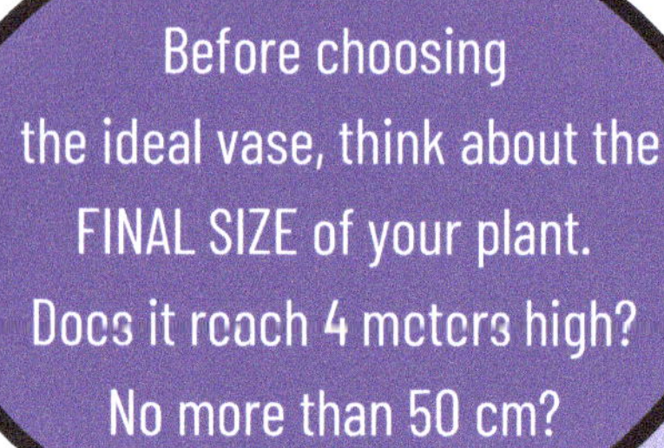

The big garden store chains infest the plants with chemical fertilisers, pesticides and fungicides so they stay beautiful until you buy them. Pay attention and avoid buying old plants. It's mostly likely going to die after you take it home.

To price your work, take into account the price of the plant, the vase, the soil, the stones, the fertiliser, your hourly work, your knowledge, promotion, rent, fuel, displacement, packaging and delivery. This is all you SPEND, not profit.

INDOOR PLANTS

CHAPTER 6
INDOOR PLANTS

These are some of the houses considered the most beautiful and expensive in the world.

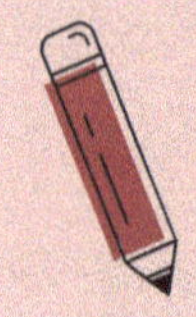

BESIDES BEING EXPENSIVE, WHAT DO THESE HOUSES HAVE IN COMMON?

____

____

Source: Mapa mundi - Google Search: "most expensive houses of the world"

Do you know what all these houses have in common? The presence of vegetation. Nowadays, we live in big cities, polluted, full of cars, with a busy routine and we live without time.

However, the period of the global pandemic, a historic moment that was previously only studied in history books, changed the scenario a little. Landscaping and gardening gained prominence. The pursuit of health, mental and physical well-being was placed first. People needed to bring harmony and peace into their homes.

And what is the best way to improve the environment in which we live? Purchasing plants and researching on "how to take care of plants at home", have never been so popular.

But what are the best indoor plants? Are there limits? What care should I have? First, let's take a test.

WHAT ARE THE CHARACTERISTICS OF PLANTS FOR INDOOR SPACES?

	✔	✘	
A.			PLANTS THAT REQUIRE A LOT OF SUNLIGHT
B.			TOXIC PLANTS
C.			PLANTS RESISTANT TO AIR CONDITIONING
D.			HIGH MAINTENANCE PLANTS
E.			INDIRECT LIGHT PLANTS
F.			PLANTS EASY TO CARE FOR
G.			LARGE PLANTS
H.			CLIMBING PLANTS
I.			PLANTS THAT ADAPT TO DIFFERENT TYPES OF CLIMATE

C - E - F - I

INDOOR PLANTS

Indoor plants should be in **partial shade**. Plants supposed to be in direct sunlight can suffer from indirect lighting, etiolate and even die.

Avoid using toxic plants indoors, where there is a greater risk of contact with animals and young children.

Most people looking for indoor plants want practicality. Look for plants that are easy to grow, for those who don't have much time.

There are plants that are more resistant to wind and dry air. These are ideal for offices, malls and air-conditioned homes.

Remember that the final size of the plant says a lot about the ideal place and vase for it. Be careful when planting an oak tree indoors.

Indoor plants are generally easier to care for. But that doesn't mean they don't need watering, pruning, fertilisation and attention.

The best indoor plants are small to medium sized potted plants.

Hanging plants are also great for shelves and bookshelves. Climbing and large plants need more space to grow.

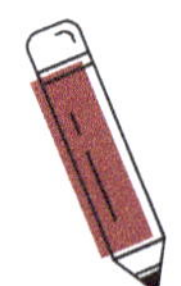

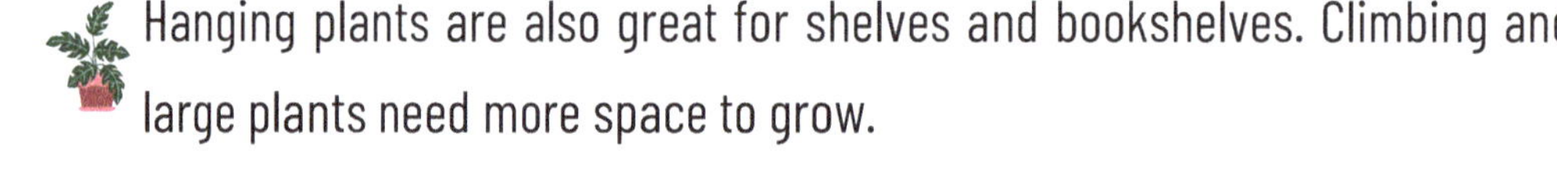

WHAT PLANTS DO YOU KNOW THAT FIT THE DESCRIPTION ABOVE?

EXPAND YOUR COLLECTION

ZAMIOCULCA

My favourite shade plant. Indirect light, spaced watering, well-draining soil. The most resistant on the list.

NATURAL HABITAT   TANZANIA, ÁFRICA
ORIGIN BIOME   TROPICAL
TOXIC PLANT   YES
SCIENTIFIC NAME   ZAMIOCULCAS ZAMIIFOLIA

RHAPIS

Great plant for offices, as it requires little care and is resistant to air conditioning. Although it resists dry weather, it is important to spray water on the leaves to prevent them from burning.

NATURAL HABITAT   CHINA, ASIA
ORIGIN BIOME   TEMPERATE
TOXIC PLANT   NO
SCIENTIFIC NAME   RHAPIS EXCELSA

SWORD FERN

Ferns appreciate humidity and frequent watering. Be careful with the strong sun and wind, which harm the humidity and burn its leaves.

NATURAL HABITAT   SOUTH AMERICA
ORIGIN BIOME   TROPICAL FOREST
TOXIC PLANT   YES
SCIENTIFIC NAME   NEPHROLEPIS EXALTATA

ANTHURIUM

Resistant plant and good for those who don't have much time. It needs indirect light and high humidity.

NATURAL HABITAT   AMAZON
ORIGIN BIOME   AMAZON FOREST
TOXIC PLANT   YES
SCIENTIFIC NAME   ANTHURIUM

DID YOU NOTICE ANY SIMILARITIES BETWEEN THE INDOOR PLANTS? OBSERVING THE CHARACTERISTICS OF THE NATURAL HABITAT: INDIRECT LIGHT AND EASY CULTIVATION.

AFRICAN VIOLET

They are perfect for gifts, as they are easy to care for. But the secret is to make it bloom again. Light and humidity.

NATURAL HABITAT   TANZANIA, ÁFRICA
ORIGIN BIOME   TROPICAL
TOXIC PLANT   YES
SCIENTIFIC NAME   SAINTPAULIA IONANTHA

CALATHEA

There are more than 150 different species. They attract attention with their foliage that appears to be hand-painted.

NATURAL HABITAT   SOUTH AMERICA
ORIGIN BIOME   TROPICAL FOREST
TOXIC PLANT   NO
SCIENTIFIC NAME   CALATHEA (VARIOUS SPECIES)

PEACE LILY

Another easy-care plant that appreciates indirect light and humidity. The strong sun burns its leaves.

NATURAL HABITAT   SOUTH AMERICA
ORIGIN BIOME   TROPICAL FOREST
TOXIC PLANT   YES
SCIENTIFIC NAME   SPATHIPHYLLUM WALLISII

SNAKE PLANT

Very practical and versatile, it is found in many places. But, for it to look really beautiful, it shouldn't be left in the sun.

NATURAL HABITAT   WEST AFRICA
ORIGIN BIOME   TROPICAL
TOXIC PLANT   YES
SCIENTIFIC NAME   SANSEVIERIA TRIFASCIATA

WHY KNOW THE SCIENTIFIC NAME OF A PLANT?

In different regions, plants have different popular names, which can cause confusion. There are also different species, in one family. Example: American fern, French lace, Hawaiian, etc.
The best way to research natural habitat and toxicity is on English-language sites.

OUTDOOR PLANTS

CHAPTER 7
OUTDOOR PLANTS

These are images of famous gardens around the world.

KEUKENHOF GARDENS, NETHERLANDS

KIRSTENBOSCH NATIONAL BOTANICAL GARDEN, SOUTH AFRICA

JARDIM BOTÂNICO, BRAZIL

KOISHIKAWA KORAKUEN, JAPAN

VERSAILLES, FRANCE

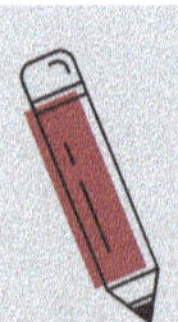

CAN YOU IDENTIFY SOMETHING IN COMMON IN THESE PICTURES?

Ah, the outdoors! When analysing the photos on the previous page, it is possible to see the colour and diversity of species that only nature knows how to create. Blossoming vegetation, vibrant colours, large sizes, trees, shrubs, vegetables, plants from arid climates, such as succulents and cacti. Most of these plants adapt best in outdoor environments, with sunlight, rain, wind and everything that nature has to offer. But that doesn't mean they don't need a gardeners' attention. Each one has its specific characteristics and care.

Now, look again at the photos of the most famous gardens in the world. I chose these to draw attention to a very important detail in gardening: Each garden is made up of **plants native** to the country.

WOULD IT BE POSSIBLE TO CREATE AN OUTDOOR TULIP GARDEN IN BRAZIL?

LET`S TALK ABOUT TULIPS?

Tulips originate from Turkey, but it was in the Netherlands that they gained fame. Today, the Dutch are the largest producers and exporters of tulips in the world. It's no wonder that the Netherlands is known for its immense fields and gardens of tulips, of all colours.

But what is the weather like in the Netherlands? Constant rain, cold and a summer that reaches a maximum of 26°C. They consider a pleasant and "not-that-cold" climate to be an average of 2°C to 5°C. Not pleasant for us Brazilians, as we would already be freezing.

The city of Holambra (Brazil) is the largest producer of tulips in Brazil. They keep tulip bulbs preserved in chambers with temperatures at -2°C. Floricultures keep the seedlings in cold chambers until it is time to sell.

After purchasing one, it is advisable to add ice cubes to preserve it.
Can you understand why a tulip garden in the heat of Brazil wouldn't work?
Remember that it's necessary to recreate the conditions of the natural habitat for the development of a species.

The same would happen if a garden of Geraniums (Pelargonium) would be planted in the northern Finland, for example. This **tropical flower** would only survive during the few months of spring and summer, having no way of surviving outdoors when the cold weather and darkness come.

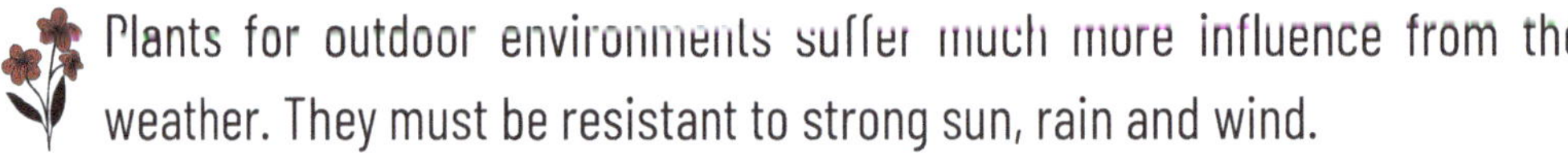

PLANTS OUTSIDE

Plants for outdoor environments suffer much more influence from the weather. They must be resistant to strong sun, rain and wind.

They normally require more care than plants that are kept indoors, as they are more exposed to pests, weeds and the actions of nature.

Not all outdoor plants like strong sun or heavy rain. Get to know each one and its characteristics.

Winter and cold? Some plants cannot withstand the cold (or snow) and need to be protected.

Are you going to create a garden or want to decorate your home? Choose plants native to the location. Adaptation will be easier, as it favours the region's ecosystem.

Want to use plants from another country? Nothing prevents a gardener from using non-native plants, but care must be taken to create ideal conditions. It's also a good idea to know about regulations of your country about non-native species.

Plants for outdoor environments can range from small to large.

You can create gardens in pots, with flowerbeds, masses of vegetation, trees, shrubs, bodies of water and much more. There are no limits to an inspired gardener.

WHAT PLANTS DO YOU KNOW THAT FIT THE DESCRIPTION ABOVE?

EXPAND YOUR COLLECTION

COMMON BOX

This is a favorite among modern landscapers,
as it can be used for barriers or marking paths.
It is easy to care for and it is possible to create
various shapes with pruning.

NATURAL HABITAT   ASIA, EUROPE
ORIGIN BIOME   TEMPERATE FOREST
TOXIC PLANT   YES
SCIENTIFIC NAME   BUXUS SEMPERVIRENS

GARDEN CROTON

This plant has uniquely coloured foliage. It
needs sun most of the day.
It is being increasingly used in businesses, as
it is practical and resistant.

NATURAL HABITAT   INDONESIA, AUSTRALIA
ORIGIN BIOME   MEADOW
TOXIC PLANT   YES (SEEDS)
SCIENTIFIC NAME   CODIAEUM VARIEGATUM

SAGO PALM

The Sago needs sun, but adapts to shade.
It stands out for its more compact size
and can even be planted in pots.

NATURAL HABITAT   SOUTH OF JAPAN, CHINA
ORIGIN BIOME   SUBTROPICAL FOREST
TOXIC PLANT   YES (SEEDS AND ROOT)
SCIENTIFIC NAME   CYCAS REVOLUTA

RUFFLED FAN PALM

Its leaves are fan-shaped.
It needs plenty of sun, but adapts to partial
shade. Does not support strong winds.

NATURAL HABITAT   SOUTHWEST OF ASIA
ORIGIN BIOME   SUBTROPICAL FOREST
TOXIC PLANT   NO
SCIENTIFIC NAME   LICUALA GRANDIS

WHAT IS SUBTROPICAL?

It is a transition from a tropical to a temperate climate, with hot summers and cold winters. That's why
the two palm trees on the list adapt so well to sun and shade, unlike other species that need sun all the
time, such as Acumã Palm (Syagrus flexuosa).

In addition, be careful when using palm trees in northern countries, as they are native to South
American and African environments and should not adapt to snowy weathers.

BASIL

Do you want to have a vegetable garden at home? Know that it needs sun and frequent watering! The best place for it is outside, but there's nothing stopping you from having one indoors if it's near the window.

NATURAL HABITAT	ASIA, AFRICA
ORIGIN BIOME	TROPICAL SAVANNAH
TOXIC PLANT	NO
SCIENTIFIC NAME	OCIMUM BASILICUM

DESERT ROSE

This plant needs sun, heat and little water. With cold and wind it loses its leaves and goes into dormancy. The flowers are beautiful and come in many colours.

NATURAL HABITAT	SOCOTRA ISLANDS (AFRICA)
ORIGIN BIOME	SAVANNAH
TOXIC PLANT	YES (SAP)
SCIENTIFIC NAME	ADENIUM OBESUM

AGAVE

This is for those who have a large garden. There are different species of Agave, which make any garden spectacular. They need constant sun and little water.

NATURAL HABITAT	MEXICO
ORIGIN BIOME	DESERT
TOXIC PLANT	YES
SCIENTIFIC NAME	AGAVE (VARIOUS SPECIES)

JONQUIL

Also called Rain Lily, precisely because its flower resembles that of the Lily, but this species appreciates sun and water. The flowers come in different shades and are very delicate.

NATURAL HABITAT	CENTRAL ASIA
ORIGIN BIOME	TEMPERATE FOREST
TOXIC PLANT	YES
SCIENTIFIC NAME	NARCISSUS JONQUILLA

HOW ABOUT BEING A LANDSCAPE GARDENER?

Did you know that you already have enough knowledge to carry out a landscaping pre-project? Choose an empty space, write down the characteristics of light, shadow, wind, rain and weather. Then propose some plants for the place, taking all of this into consideration. This is the first step of a landscaping project!

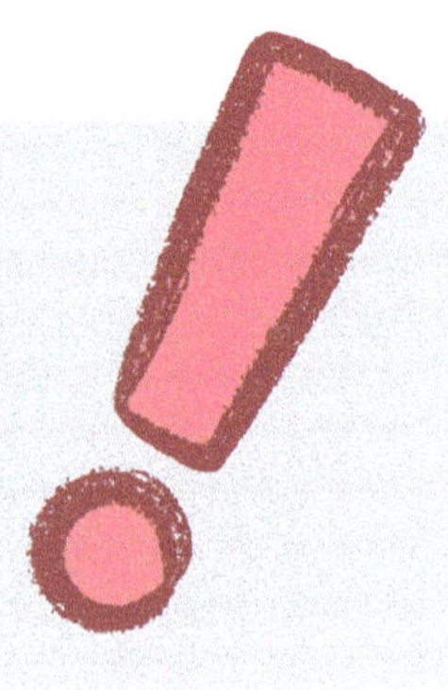

FLOWERS, FLOWERS!

CHAPTER 8
FLOWERS, FLOWERS!

This is the most colourful and fragrant chapter in this book. They are beautiful, have different shapes, scents and colours to attract pollinators, but that's not all: they are the plant's reproductive organs.

HOW DO PLANTS REPRODUCE?

Nature is so wise that we find both male and female reproductive organs in a single flower. The female part of the plant — the ovary — is called the **Gynoecium**. The male organ is the pollen, called **Androecium**.

And how does Androecium get to Gyneceus?

By the wind or by the action of **pollinating agents**, such as bees, wasps, butterflies, beetles, birds and bats. Landing on the flower, in search of food, these pollinators fill themselves with pollen, spreading it to other places.

From the fertilisation of the reproductive organs, seeds are formed, these seeds fall to the ground and new plants are born. A perfect cycle.

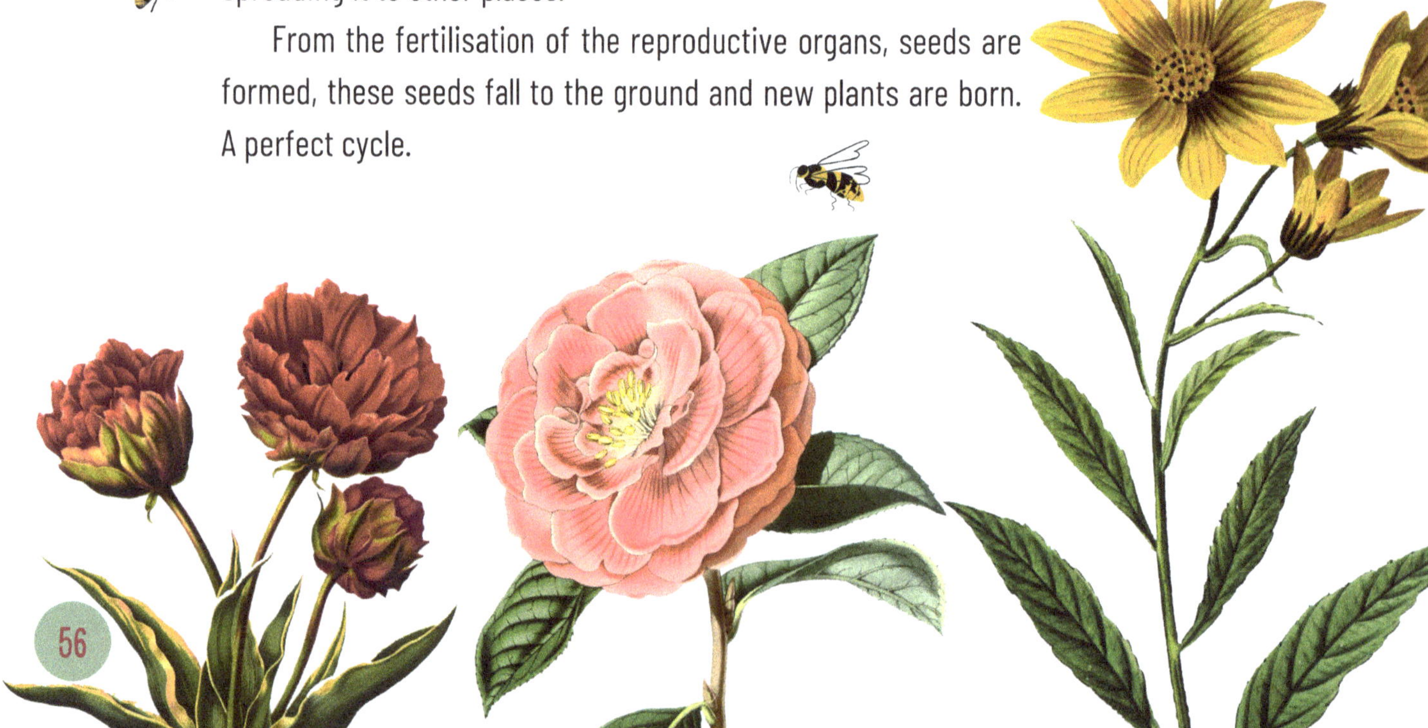

FLOWERING

Have you ever bought a beautiful, flowering plant and it never bloomed again? It happens to the best of gardeners. However, it is important to follow some techniques to ensure flowering every year. First, let's see what factors prevent flowering.

PESTS

Pests are a sign that something is not going well with your plant. Furthermore, they drain the energy necessary for flowering.

LACK OF LIGHT

The biggest cause of plants not flowering is inadequate lighting. Abundant light is the key to flowers every year.

LACK OF PRUNING

Plants distribute their energies to all their parts. If there is no pruning, the strength needed for flowering is taken away by old, dry leaves.

LACK OF FERTILISER

Plants need nutrients for flowering, especially **phosphorus**.

FLOWERING TIME

There are plants that only bloom in spring, others in autumn, others all year round. Know the flowering time of each one to know the right time to fertilise and prune.

DEHYDRATION

Without watering, there are no flowers. Water is responsible for photosynthesis, hydration and nutrient absorption.

TEMPERATURE

Temperatures that are too high or too low prevent flowering.

BLOSSOMING SEASON

Ever wondered why spring is the season for flowers? This happens because this time of year has climate, light and rain conditions that stimulate flowering. However, it is not just in spring that we must take some precautions. To ensure flowering every year, know the characteristics of each season and what each one requires:

Spring is the time that most favours plant growth. It's time for pruning (if not done in winter), fertilising, growing new plants and increasing the frequency of watering.

In summer, plants are more exposed to strong sunlight and may suffer from burns. Avoid watering plants under the sun (it might damage the plant) and if it's a potted plant it might be worth giving it some protection against the sun.

In autumn, the leaves begin to lose some of their colour, as they are concentrating their energy to withstand the winter cold. It's the perfect time to prune old, dry leaves. Place your plants in a brighter location.

The tropical winter is not as severe as the winter in countries in the northern hemisphere. There is no snow, nor freezing temperatures. But even so, the weaker sun and low temperatures are a magnet for pests and fungi. Keep your plants closer to the light and prune them well.

FROZEN

If you live in a snowy country, you deserve a whole different look into your garden and how to make your plants survive during winter. In Scandinavian winter, when temperatures drop to -30°C, or less, it's basically impossible to grow anything outdoors, if not native needle trees and taiga or tundra vegetation.

For this reason, if you want to grow plants all year, they need to be indoors - or at least be placed indoors or in a greenhouse at the first sign of autumn. The **flowers and other vegetation** from warmer climates will die. The deciduous vegetation (that will drop their leaves) and grass will mostly liked grow again next spring. But most vegetation that is outdoors will need to be replanted.

Put everything you wanna keep alive inside and protected from cold. It is better to keep them by the windows, to get as much sunlight as possible, and to make use of heat LED lightbulbs. They will keep the photosynthesis process in your plant going, preventing its death. But you might only expect blossoming next spring, as they will be put in a **natural slumber during winter**.

FLOWERS FOR THE WINTER

SOME SPECIES TO KEEP YOUR GARDEN COLOURFUL, EVER DURING A WHITE, SNOWY WINTER.
THEY BLOSSOM VERY EARLY IN SPRING AND LATE AUTUMN, EVEN WITH SOME SNOW ON THE GROUND.

SNOWDROPS

NATURAL HABITAT	EUROPE
ORIGIN BIOME	TAIGA
TOXIC PLANT	YES
SCIENTIFIC NAME	GALANTHUS

WINTERBERRY

NATURAL HABITAT	NORTH AMERICA
ORIGIN BIOME	TAIGA
TOXIC PLANT	YES (TO HUMANS)
SCIENTIFIC NAME	ILEX VERTICILLATA

GLORY OF THE SNOW

NATURAL HABITAT	TURKEY
ORIGIN BIOME	TEMP. FOREST
TOXIC PLANT	YES
SCIENTIFIC NAME	CHIONODOXA LUCILIAE

WINTER ACONITE

NATURAL HABITAT	FRANCE, ITALY
ORIGIN BIOME	TEMP. FOREST
TOXIC PLANT	YES
SCIENTIFIC NAME	ERANTHIS HYEMALIS

One of the main factors for flowering is photoperiodism. The number of hours a plant receives light, versus the number of hours at night.

In spring, these two periods are about the same, 12h/12h, which is ideal.

Fertilisation is essential for flowering. Some nutrients, such as phosphorus, are the main agents that make the plant produce flowers. They can be easily found in organic fertilisers, such as bone meal.

It is important to properly hydrate your plants. Whenever the soil is completely dry, water abundantly.

Some plants prefer moist soil, others can handle a longer dry period. But, they all need irrigation.

Pruning is essential for flowering. But, they must be done at the right time. After flowering, general pruning must be done. In other seasons, pruning of old and dry leaves should be done, and also to allow sunlight into the most hidden parts of the plant, if necessary.

FRUIT TREES

CHAPTER 9
FRUIT TREES

Have you ever thought about having your own fruit production at home? You can grow fruit trees on the sidewalk, in the backyard or even in pots on the balcony! In this chapter, you will learn about fruit-tree care in smaller spaces. It is possible to grow any fruit tree at home, as long as ideal conditions are created for its development.

Believe me, space is the least of your problems. What you really need is abundant lighting. You can get grafted trees in order to grow smaller trees in your garden and even in pots. However, it is still a tree and it will require the same amount of light and irrigation a normal-sized tree would.

BASIC RULES OF CULTIVATION

 Watering should be frequent in hot weather. Try to water your tree at times when the sun is lower.

 Fruit trees should receive sun most of the day.

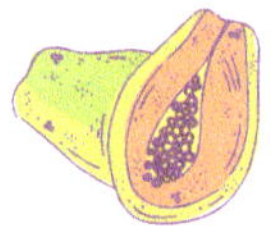 Do not use any type of chemical product. Use organic pesticides and fertilisers instead.

 Give preference to ceramic vases, with plenty of room for your tree.

 Look for grafted seedlings from **good producers**.

DRAINAGE

The pot you choose must have holes and a good drainage layer. Use expanded clay, pebbles, and a drainage blanket for good water drainage.

Don't make the mistake of planting your tree in pots without holes. Remember that watering is almost daily (depending on environmental conditions) and the chances of waterlogging are high.

CLIMATE

There is a reason why passion fruit is very expensive in Sweden and blueberries are very expensive in Brazil. Fruit trees also have an appropriate climate where they can grow and bear fruit throughout the year.

If you plan on having a banana tree in Scandinavia, know that you will have to do so in a greenhouse. The same goes for your blueberry bush that would burn under the Brazilian sun.

LIGHTING

Fruit trees need full sun. Therefore, the ideal place for it is outside the house, in the sunniest place you can find.

Does your house not have a good place for it? Invest in another type of plant, or fruit trees that accept a shadier location, such as blackberries, raspberries or strawberries, which are ideal for northern countries.

VASE

Know the final size of your tree to choose the pot. An orange tree requires a pot larger than a strawberry plant. Another example: an avocado tree needs a larger pot than an orange tree.

Remember that grafted trees do not grow as much as seeded ones, and are recommended for planting in pots.

FERTILISING

Fertilisation must be done frequently. Always give preference to organic fertilisers. Fertilisation rich in potassium favours fruiting.

But do not exaggerate. Excessive fertilisation kills a plant faster than the lack of it.

FRUITS

What can I plant? Any fruit! Know the flowering and fruiting season of your tree, plant it at the right time and get ready to harvest fruit in your home. Learn about the climate it adapts best to.

I recommend grafted trees, which will bear fruit within a year. Seeded trees take many years to reach adulthood and bear fruit.

LARGE FRUIT TREES

BE GENEROUS WITH THAT VASE, ALRIGHT?

- Avocado.
- Mango.
- Guava.
- Banana.

MEDIUM SIZED FRUIT TREES

IDEAL FOR BALCONIES AND BACKYARDS.

- Orange.
- Lime.
- Mulberry.
- Raspberry.
- Surinam Cherry.

SMALL FRUIT TREES

FITS ANYWHERE!

- Pear.
- Strawberry plant.
- Blueberry bush.
- Passion fruit tree (you only need a tutor for it to grow, as it becomes a vine).

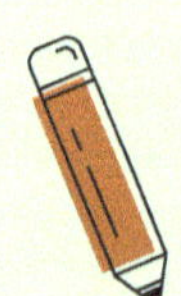 WHAT FRUIT TREES WOULD YOU LIKE TO GROW?

____

____

URBAN JUNGLE

CHAPTER 10
URBAN JUNGLE

If you like plants, you probably have heard of this term in English "urban jungle". This trend comes from the lack of green and **open spaces** in large cities, where humans needed to find a way to bring nature closer.

It is no surprise that, in America, the large flow of people during the holidays is towards the beach or countryside — not the other way around.

But this phenomenon is not by chance. Before great civilizations, human beings lived amidst nature and, even after the entire process of evolution and globalisation, this relationship is still installed in our DNA.

Being connected with green is in our essence. Therefore, we feel calm, relaxed and welcomed, with the slightest presence of nature in our environment. It gives us the feeling of being at home.

WHAT IS URBAN JUNGLE? WHO SAID THAT A SMALL SPACE INDOORS CANNOT HAVE VEGETATION?

If you are a European, you're probably used to arboured streets and having a forest or park close to home. In America things are a bit different. If that's where you are from, there's a good chance you know someone who bought a potted plant for their living room, and months later their house looks like a forest.

People need to be surrounded by green, and that need has made this trend increasingly strong among landscapers, gardeners and plant owners.

With each passing day, we live in smaller and smaller houses, with small or even non-existent backyards. The solution is to create green spaces within four walls. Vases (of all sizes), planters, shelves, railings and panels. Anything goes to create your own urban jungle.

CREATE YOUR OWN URBAN JUNGLE

 Always choose species that adapt to your type of environment. There is no point in planting a full sun palm tree in a room without natural light. Foliage is more suitable for an urban jungle than flowers, as its maintenance is simpler.

 Vases of different sizes and colour tones always make interesting combinations.

 Choose vases and stands that match your decor. There are a variety of models and materials. Cement, ceramics, glass, wood, plastic, polyethylene... The options are countless.

 Try to recreate the natural habitat of the chosen vegetation as far as possible. In general, tropical plants stay in the shade, while those in arid climates will need more sun.

 Try to place your plants in the space you use the most. So, in addition to making it more cosy, you don't forget to water them.

 Vertical gardens are a great choice for those who don't have space. Shelves, wall brackets, trellises, panels, plant hangers and nets can be used to create an amateur vertical garden.

Want something more sophisticated? A landscaper can design a self-irrigating garden, making your urban jungle even more pleasant.

WHAT PLANTS WOULD YOU LIKE TO HAVE IN YOUR URBAN JUNGLE?

VEGETABLE GARDEN

CHAPTER 11
VEGETABLE GARDEN

Have you noticed how organic foods are much more expensive on supermarket shelves? Fresh products, grown without the use of agrochemicals, pesticides, organically and sustainably fertilised are much healthier and of better quality.

The number of people seeking a more organic way of life is growing every day. This is an excellent reason for plant lovers to grow their own food at home and start a vegetable garden.

Anyone who thinks that it takes a lot of space and technique to cultivate a vegetable garden is mistaken. Everything can be grown, as long as it is in a suitable place: With abundant sunlight, irrigation and natural ventilation.

From vases on the wall to beds on the floor, there are countless possibilities for a vegetable garden, of the most varied sizes.

Choose the sunniest place in your home, some pots (at least a diameter of 20 centimeters), plant some seedlings of your favorite herbs, water daily and watch your garden develop. Practical and uncomplicated.

In chapters 13 and 14, you'll learn more about irrigation and the best type of soil for your vegetable garden.

WHAT TO PLANT?

 MEDICINAL HERBS
EDIBLE PLANTS
HERBS
FRUIT TREES
SPICES
GREENS
VEGETABLES
FRUITS

 TOXIC PLANTS

TYPES OF VEGETABLE GARDENS

IN VASES

Don't have space? With pots starting at 20 centimeters, you can now grow herbs and spices. How about putting them by the window?

PERFECT FOR IT BASIL, ROSEMARY, PARSLEY, PEPPER, CHIVES, MINT.

IN A VERTICAL GARDEN

Larger vegetables require more space, this does not mean you cannot plant them in planters. There are different models and materials.

PERFECT FOR IT STRAWBERRY, LETTUCE, CABBAGE, LAVENDER, TOMATO.

IN THE SOIL

Do you want to have a bigger garden, with fruit trees and a variety of vegetables? If you have space, choose to grow your vegetable garden in the ground, where it can develop.

PERFECT FOR IT POTATOES, PASSION FRUIT, CARROTS, FRUIT TREES.

IN GARDEN BEDS

Garden beds also offer more space, but they don't have to be on the ground. You can build a raised bed and fill it with soil. Ideal for those who have animals that love to destroy their crops, as it can be high or fenced.

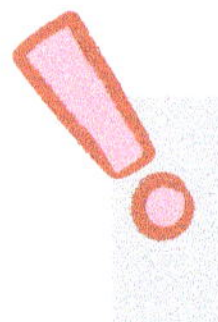

ARE YOU INTO RECYCLING?

For the more sustainable gardeners, it is possible to create vegetable gardens by reusing empty plastic bottles, market crates and even toilet paper rolls. Use your imagination!

SUN OR SHADOW?

CHAPTER 12
SUN OR SHADOW?

This is the first question you should ask when buying a new plant at the garden store: "Is it a plant for the sun or shade?" At the end of this chapter you will know where to place your plant and what type of lighting it needs to thrive.

Before understanding more about the subject, do you know what problems can arise with inadequate lighting?

 **QUICK TEST!** 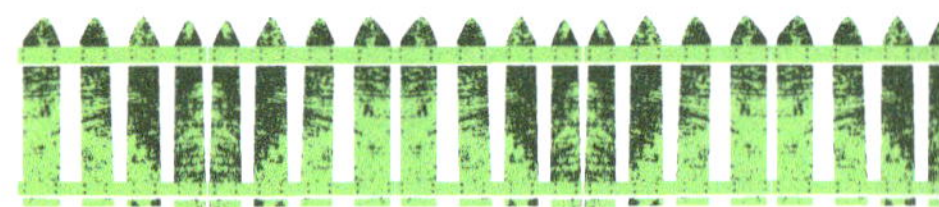

What problems below are directly related to lighting and solar incidence?

A. WHITISH AND PALE LEAVES.

B. WITHERED LEAVES.

C. ETIOLATION AND ACCELERATED GROWTH.

D. COMPACTED SOIL.

E. BURNT LEAVES.

F. CURLED LEAVES.

G. TOO MANY DEAD LEAVES.

H. FUNGI AND PESTS.

I. LACK OF FLOWERS AND FRUITS.

A-C-E-H-I

INADEQUATE LIGHTING

FUNGI
LACK OF LIGHTING

FUNGI
LACK OF LIGHTING

PALE LEAVES
LACK OF LIGHTING

BURNT FLOWERS
EXCESSIVE SUNLIGHT

ETIOLATION
LACK OF SUNLIGHT

ETIOLATION / SPACED LEAVES
LACK OF SUNLIGHT

COCHINEAL
LACK OF SUNLIGHT

BURNT LEAVES
EXCESSIVE SUNLIGHT

DO YOU REMEMBER?

As we saw in chapter 4, leaves give out several signals about the health of the plant.

To the side, we see examples of vegetation that received inadequate amounts of light. The **absence of natural light** directly interferes with photosynthesis and chlorophyll production, which gives the green pigment to the leaves — leaving them pale and lifeless.

This is also a big reason for the **appearance of pests and fungi**, which multiply more easily in shaded environments. The lack of light causes plants to produce less energy, making them weaker and susceptible to disease attacks. **Such weakening is also the reason why your plant never flowers or bear fruit**.

However, you are wrong if you think that leaving the plant in direct sunlight solves all these problems. **Excessive sunlight can also harm more sensitive plants**, which will soon show brownish, burnt and dry leaves.

Let's do an exercise! You will see how simple it is to choose the ideal location for each plant. Imagine you went to a garden store and bought two new plants:

A **Monstera Deliciosa** seedling and a pot of **Geranium**. That's what you bought at the garden store. Now you're at home and you have no idea whether these are sun or shade plants. Before searching the internet and being bombarded with information — which is not always correct — read this chapter and decide where you are going to place your new plants later.

 ❶ FULL SUN

Most full sun plants have lighter and more colourful leaves, have **visible and exuberant** flowering and their natural habitat is often sunny places, such as the savannah, desert or temperate climates.

What are full sun plants

Plants that must be exposed to direct sunlight for **6 or more hours daily** and do not adapt to shadowy places.

This type of vegetation is ideal for outdoor areas and gardens, but it also adapts well to windows or balconies.

Pay attention to whether your plant is receiving direct sunlight most of the day or just light. If you see signs, expose it more and more to the sun until you find the ideal spot.

What are partial shade plants

Plants that should be exposed to **weak sunlight for 4 hours** and indirect light for the rest of the day.

Partial shade plants are those that adapt to both **outdoor and indoor** environments. They are generally native to **temperate climates, and not extreme biomes**. Therefore, they should not be placed in the hot sun, nor in very dark places.

It is important to always pay attention to the signs that the plant shows if it needs more or less light. Be careful with those that are on the dining table or hanging very close to the ceiling, **they may not be receiving as much light as you imagine**.

③ SHADOW

The first thing you should know is: **There is no such thing as total shade vegetation**. With the exception of those that live at the bottom of the ocean, every living being needs light to develop. Therefore, even shade plants should be exposed to **weak morning sun rays**.

What are shadow plants

Plants that are more resistant and should only be exposed to **weak morning sunlight for 2 hours**.

Remember that shade is not synonymous of darkness and look for a place with indirect light if you want them to develop and bloom again. Tropical, dark-coloured vegetation (and others that are used to humid and shaded environments) are perfect for indoors or spaces, under trees or pergolas.

Now let's go back to the two plants you bought and choose the ideal place for them? Consider the information above about each plant and what you learned about sun and shade.

WHERE WOULD YOU PLACE YOUR NEW PLANTS?

✔ The Monstera adapts best in 3-4, while the Geranium should be between 1-2.

IRRIGATION

CHAPTER 13
IRRIGATION

This is undoubtedly the main reason why your plants die from one moment to the next: **inadequate irrigation**. The rule is that all vegetation need water to complete all of its cycles and produce energy, but in what quantity? You have already learned the symptoms of excessive or insufficient watering. Now it's time to know how to water correctly.

The truth is that it doesn't make a difference. The issue here is practicality.

If you have a large garden and large plants, there is no reason to water them with a glass of water. Likewise, it doesn't make sense to water your indoor plants with a hose.

The secret is knowing how much water each plant needs and knowing when to stop. In general, plants that are exposed to full sun require frequent watering (depending on where you live, even twice a day), while indoor plants should not be watered more than two or three times a week.

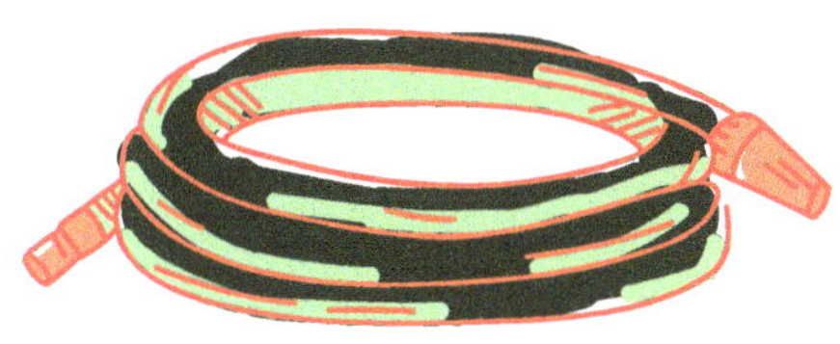

TAKE NOTES!

Place your finger or a toothpick in the substrate and see if it is still damp (until you understand the frequency of watering needed). If it's wet, wait a few more days. If it is dry, water abundantly.

As a gardener, I must tell you that it is not advisable to use pots without holes for your plants. **Especially those in the shade**. To avoid the accumulation of water in the roots (consequently rotting of the plant), lack of oxygen in the soil, and the multiplication of fungi and pests; a good drainage system is essential.

When you water, all excess water is drained and your plant absorbs only what it needs. This doesn't happen in a vase without holes, where everything gets puddled.

IT'S A SIMPLE SOLUTION!

If you want to plant directly in that pretty cachepot you bought, make holes in it. Any drill or nail will solve the problem.

But if you choose not to drill holes in it (or if it is made of glass), pay much more attention to watering, only watering when the substrate is completely dry and bring your vase closer to natural light.

Spraying water on your plant's leaves is not the same as watering it. With the first, you maintain air humidity, preventing the leaves from drying out and burning, as well as some fungi and pests. By watering, you hydrate and ensure the functionality of all plant systems.

Some plants of tropical origin, for example, must be sprayed daily in order to imitate the climate of tropical forests. At the same time, watering should be done according to your custom.

GARDENER'S TIP

Foliage often appreciates water sprayed on its leaves.

Tropical plants such as Ferns, Raphis, Monstera, Money plant, etc., can be sprayed daily. This will prevent those leaves getting burnt tips, due to the dry weather.

Is there an optimal time of the day to water your plants or not? Yes, away from strong sunlight. Any irrigation close to midday will cook the roots and leave stains on the leaves.

The ideal is to water very early in the morning, as there is a whole day for the excess water to drain and evaporate.

Late afternoon is also a good time to irrigate your garden, for those who don't have time to do it in the morning.

NIGHTTIME WATERING

Watering at night is also a good alternative to avoid the hottest times.

However, pay extra attention to the accumulation of water and excess humidity. This is a recipe for the appearance of fungi and pests.

SOIL

CHAPTER 14
SOIL

Choosing the ideal type of substrate or correcting the soil in which you are going to grow is an essential skill for any gardener — amateur or professional. It is the soil that will be responsible for nourishing, fixating and protecting your garden.

Unless you prefer hydroponics (growing in water), you need to understand what types of soil there are and how to create the best substrate for each plant.

Let's find out what substrates are most commonly found in gardening stores. We'll also take a look at some mixes to use in your garden.

TYPES OF SOIL SUBSTRATE

SANDY

This is the ideal substrate for succulents, vegetable gardens and plants in general.   The earth is mixed with sand, making the soil sandy and well-oxygenated.

CLAYISH

Also known as brown- or red earth. It has a high concentration of clay in its composition, therefore, it retains more water and contains fewer nutrients. It is not suitable for planting and must be corrected.

HUMUS

Result of the decomposition of organic remains, very rich in nutrients. It is sold ready-made in a garden stores (don't worry, it comes without worms).

MANURE

Decomposed manure is rich in nitrogen and great for fertiliser. Either cattle or chicken are ideal for a substrate mix.

VERMICULITE

In addition to absorbing excessive moisture from the soil, it ensures aeration, preventing the substrate from becoming too compacted.

LIMESTONE

It contains calcium and other essential nutrients. Dolomite stones have high concentrations of limestone, which helps to control soil pH.

COAL

Mineral charcoal is ideal for indoor plants, as it filters water, prevents soil and roots from rotting, and prevents the appearance of fungi.

BARK AND ROCKS

Some plants do not require land and are able to attach themselves and nourish themselves on rocks and tree bark. As is the case with some orchids, for example.

MY FAVORITE SUBSTRATE MIXES

YOU MAY FIND MOST OF THESE SUBSTRATES IN GARDEN- OR FISH STORES, AS SOME OF THEM ARE USED TO MAINTAIN THE WATER IN AQUARIUMS AND TERRARIUMS.

GENERAL PLANTS- AND VEGETABLE GARDENS

ARE YOU GOING TO USE ANOTHER TYPE OF FERTILISER? REDUCE THE AMOUNT OF HUMUS.

- 5 parts of soil
- 3 parts of sand
- 2 parts humus
- 2 parts crushed charcoal

FOR SUCCULENTS

BE CAREFUL WITH CLAYEY SOIL WITHOUT AERATION.

- 3 parts of sand
- 2 parts vermeculite
- 2 parts charcoal
- 2 parts humus or manure
- 1 part of crushed bark or rocks (shells, dolomites, pine bark, etc.)

FOR SOIL CORRECTION

REMOVE APPROXIMATELY 20 CM OF SOIL AND MIX THE NEW SUBSTRATE BEFORE PLANTING!

- 5 parts of vegetable soil
- 5 parts humus or manure
- 2 parts limestone

The measures of each "part" mentioned above will depend on the amount of soil you need. For a small vase, 5 cups of soil should be enough. In the case of a whole flower bed, you might have to measure in sacks of soil, for example.

GARDENING TECHNIQUES

CHAPTER 15
GARDENING TECHNIQUES

Whenever we buy a new plant, some steps must be taken to assure that it develops correctly in the new environment. One of these measures is replanting, which is nothing more than changing the pot, giving more space for its roots and a new substrate.

In the previous chapter, you learned the importance of an aerated and well-nourished substrate. Furthermore, there are other important layers for your plant when we think about planting. But before learning how to set up your pot, let's see what types of planting you can do.

REPLANTING

Replanting is necessary when the pot can no longer accommodate the size of the plant, its roots are tight, the old substrate is already compacted and has no nutrients.

When replanting, be careful with the roots when extracting the plant. Avoid replanting during flowering season.

CUTTING

It may seem like a very difficult technique, but the concept of cutting is very simple.

Cuttings can be made using the leaf, stem, or branches of an adult and already developed plant. If pruning a branch (for example), place it to root in water or soil until the roots are 20cm or longer. After rooting, the new seedling is ready to be planted in another pot.

Attention: Not every plant is capable of multiplying by cuttings. However, it is the technique most used by gardeners to create new seedlings.

SEEDLINGS

Did you buy a seedling already developed in a bag or in a pot? Always replant to renew the substrate and nutrients.

SEEDS

Whether purchased in bags or taken from the fruit you just ate, planting seeds will always be the most common form of planting.

Plant the seeds and cover them with a maximum of 2cm of soil. They must always remain moist for germination to occur, so water them daily, or create a greenhouse to maintain humidity.

After a few days you will notice new shoots emerging. When you notice that the new seedlings are already more than 10cm tall (or more than 4 leaves) it is time to replant them in the final pot. Give it a substrate rich in nutrients!

BULB

Some plants like tulips and lilies, for example, reproduce again from bulbs. Always replant them after flowering.

It doesn't matter what type of pot or substrate you choose — for plants to adapt to the environment and develop properly, some layers are essential.

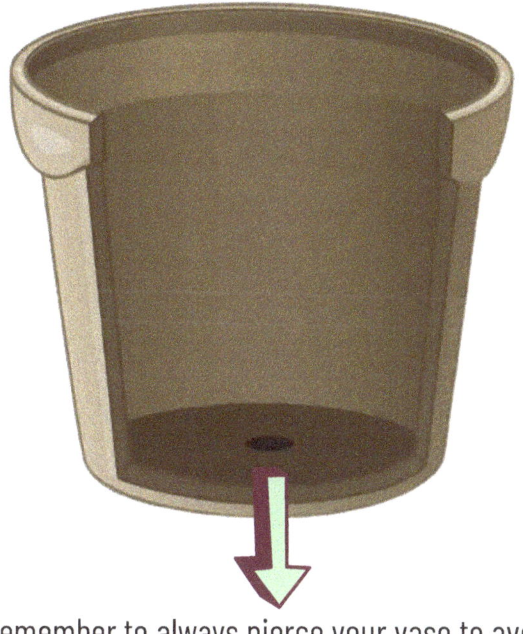

Remember to always pierce your vase to avoid water accumulation.

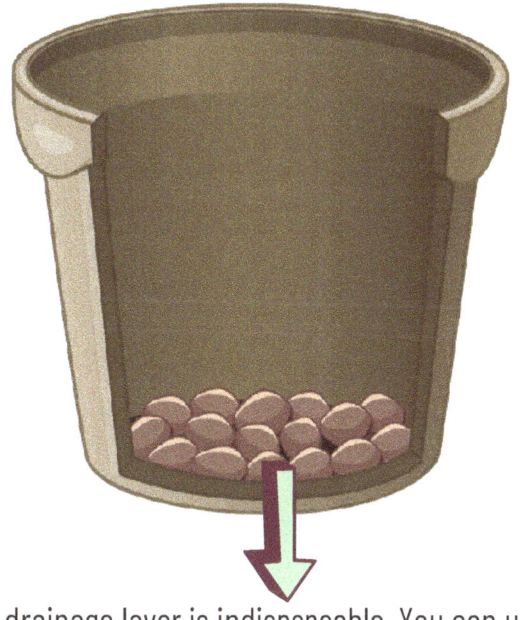

The drainage layer is indispensable. You can use any drainable material, such as expanded clay, stones, gravel and even tiles or pieces of polystyrene foam.

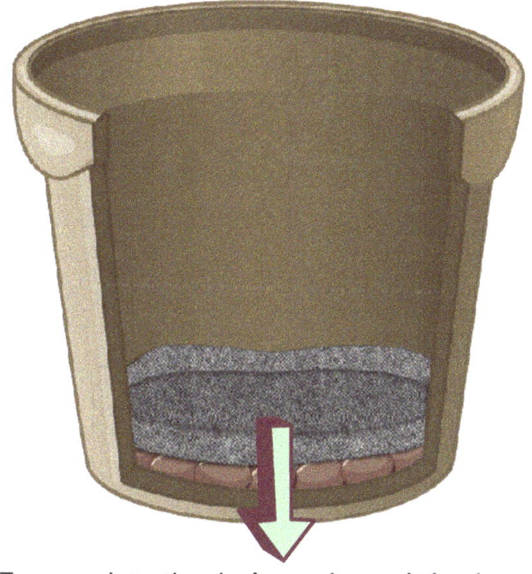

To complete the drainage layer, it is also worth adding a protective drainage blanket, woven fabric or even a porous dish cloth to protect the root and allow excess water to pass through.

Add a layer of your best substrate mixture and fertilise it. Plant and top up with the rest of the substrate.

I sketched a cut flower pot to show you what a basic soil layer should be. After taking care of the layers, there should be space for your plant to grow.

Always take the final size of the plant into consideration when choosing the pot. **Give the roots room to grow**.

After planting, the last layer is the **covering**. Straws, stones, gravel, bark, dry branches and even moss or grass are great for protecting the soil and keeping the plant moist — especially for vegetable gardens.

IN THE SOIL

Are you going to plant in the ground? The drainage layer is unnecessary, in this case, since excess water is absorbed and drained into the soil naturally.

However, if the location is not suitable, it is worth cleaning it thoroughly, correcting the soil and even placing a protective blanket to prevent the growth of weeds.

COMPOST

OR

FERTILISER

CHAPTER 16
COMPOST OR FERTILISER

You already know the importance of fertilising and nourishing your garden. However, have you ever found yourself standing in front of the fertiliser shelf at the garden store, not knowing what to buy?

This chapter will teach you the difference between compost and industrial fertiliser, and which one you should choose for your plants.

ORGANIC X INDUSTRIALISED

That old story that everything organic is healthier? In gardening it couldn't be more true. Compost is all **organic vegetable or animal matter** which, after decomposing, becomes food for plants. Food, animal remains, cereals, vegetables, mineral flours, dry leaves and manure: everything that was alive serves as compost.

Industrial fertilisers on the other hand are chemical products, which contain high concentrations of NPK (Nitrogen, Phosphorus and Potassium), but bring many harms to your garden, such as:

 It does not contain all the nutrients necessary for the full development of the plant, leaving it deficient in essential nutrients, causing the multiplication of pests and fungi.

 They can be toxic to animals and children. Therefore, they should never be used on vegetable gardens and edible plants.

 They leave the plant "addicted" to chemicals. The more you use, the more it will need. Over time, overfertilising will end up killing your plant.

 They pollute the soil and environment.

RIGHT TIME TO FERTILISE?

COMPLETE FERTILISATION

Complete fertilisation of your garden, that is, with all the essential nutrients (approx. 20 different nutrients), should be done every 3 months, depending on the fertiliser you choose.

Mineral-based fertilisers are normally slow-release, taking 2 to 3 months to need renewal.

In the case of fertilisers of animal and vegetable origin — humus, for example — decomposition is faster, and fertilisation can be done monthly.

FLOWERING

For ornamental plants that flower, know the flowering time and try to fertilise one month beforehand.

Nutrients such as phosphorus and potassium are essential during this period. Banana peel ash is a good fertiliser rich in these elements.

PREVENTION OF DISEASES

The most dry and humid times of the year (winter and summer) are also the most favourable for the appearance and multiplication of fungi and pests.

Before this period, it is worth applying a simple fertiliser, with just a few nutrients responsible for protecting and fortifying plants, such as calcium, sulphur and phosphorus.

Don't know where to find these elements? Eggshells and dark greens.

BETWEEN SEASONS

A change in weather is always a good indication that your garden is about to enter a new stage. Some plants will flower, others will bear fruit, others will go dormant or even need special care.

For those new to fertilising, scheduling a nutrient replacement at the change of seasons is a great alternative and guarantees a healthy garden all year round.

WINTER

There is a lot of talk about fertilisation in winter. Most plants are in a dormant period and therefore nutrient absorption is low or almost zero.

However, for countries where the winter is not so harsh, remember that some plants have winter as their flowering period.

Try to fertilise before winter starts to protect your garden. For plants that go into total dormancy (lose their leaves or stop growing), avoid fertilising them.

SUCCULENTS

CHAPTER 17
SUCCULENTS

There's a good chance you own a succulent. They became famous after the growth of Urban Jungles in big cities, as they are small, easy to care for and survive even the most inattentive gardeners.

Succulents, in general, have hot and arid places as their natural habitat — such as deserts, for example. Therefore, it is to be expected that the vast **majority of succulents** prefer full sun or partial shade.

Succulent is the name popularly given to these small chubby plants, however, it is any plant that has a larger reserve of water and nutrients in its leaves and stems. Due to scarcity of water and poor soil, this type of vegetation is capable of storing them, allowing them to survive in places with extreme climates.

Therefore, watering and fertilising succulents must be done carefully, **without exaggeration and only when necessary**.

 **DO YOU KNOW HOW TO GROW SUCCULENTS?** 

A. ☐ ☐ SUCCULENTS PREFER SHADED PLACES AND LITTLE NATURAL LIGHT.

B. ☐ ☐ I SHOULD FERTILISE MY SUCCULENT EVERY 15 DAYS.

C. ☐ ☐ I MUST WATER MY SUCCULENT DAILY.

D. ☐ ☐ CACTI ARE CONSIDERED SUCCULENTS.

E. ☐ ☐ SUCCULENTS PREFER A MORE AERATED SUBSTRATE.

F. ☐ ☐ FERTILISATION MUST BE DONE EVERY 3 MONTHS TO PREVENT DISEASES.

G. ☐ ☐ I SHOULD ONLY WATER MY SUCCULENT WHEN THE SOIL IS DRY.

H. ☐ ☐ SUCCULENTS DON'T FLOWER.

I. ☐ ☐ I SHOULD PRUNE MY SUCCULENT ONCE A MONTH.

D - E - F - G

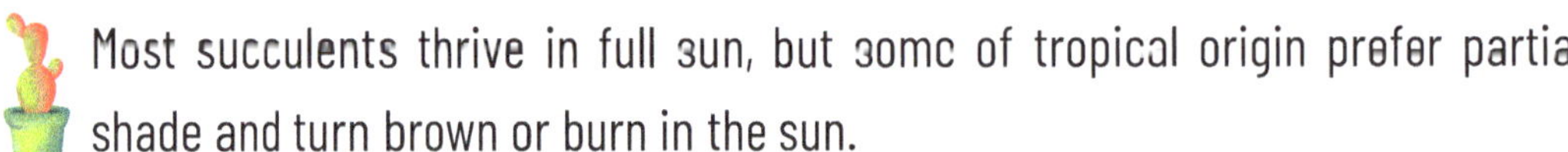

SUCCULENTS

Most succulents thrive in full sun, but some of tropical origin prefer partial shade and turn brown or burn in the sun.

All cacti (cactaceae family) are full sun and need a lot of natural light.

If you are in doubt, keep in mind that colourful, reddish, light, whitish succulents and cacti in general are in full sun. On the other hand, dark green succulents generally prefer shade.

The main symptoms of inadequate lighting are etiolation (abnormal and accelerated growth towards the light), abnormal colour change and the infestation of pests and fungi.

Avoid using pots without holes for succulents, as their roots rot easily with excess water. Watering should only be done when the substrate is completely dry.

Even though they are plants that require less fertilisation and care, you need to replace the nutrients at least every 3 months, to prevent diseases and ensure the development of your plant.

All succulents flower once a year, if they are in the right location and are properly fertilised. However, not all flowers are showy and the stems absorb a lot of the plant's energy. Always prune dry flower stems and leaves.

WHAT ARE YOUR FAVOURITE SUCCULENTS?

EXPAND YOUR COLLECTION

ECHEVERIA

There are several species of Echeverias. They are very common and recommended for beginners in cultivation.

NATURAL HABITAT — MEXICO DESERT AREAS
LIGHTING — FULL SUN
SCIENTIFIC NAME — ECHEVERIA

ALOE ARISTATA

Shade succulent, which loses its green colour if exposed to the sun. Take extra care with watering.

NATURAL HABITAT — SOUTH AFRICA
LIGHTING — SHADOW
SCIENTIFIC NAME — ALOE ARISTATA

STRING OF PEARLS

This is a hanging succulent and is more resistant to water, as it is of tropical origin. Keep the soil always moist, but not overly moist.

NATURAL HABITAT — ROCKY AREAS OF SOUTH AFRICA
LIGHTING — HALF SHADE
SCIENTIFIC NAME — SENECIO ROWLEYANUS

JADE PLANT

Resistant plant that takes on a reddish tone when exposed to the sun. It becomes a small shrub if planted in the ground.

NATURAL HABITAT — TROPICAL AND SUBTROPICAL
LIGHTING — FULL SUN
SCIENTIFIC NAME — CRASSULA OVATA

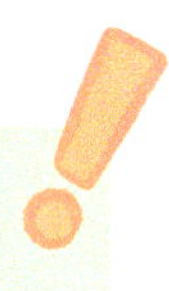

Did you notice how the species' natural habitat directly interferes with the type of lighting and care it needs? Always research the origin of your succulent!

HAWORTHIA

This is in the category of more delicate succulent species. Leave it in the shade and it takes on a transparent colour.

NATURAL HABITAT SOUTH AFRICA
LIGHTING SHADOW
SCIENTIFIC NAME HAWORTHIA

ALOE JUVENNA

With leaves that look like small teeth, this succulent prefers the shade and burns easily when exposed to the sun.

NATURAL HABITAT JUNGLES OF KENYA - AFRICA
LIGHTING SHADOW
SCIENTIFIC NAME ALOE JUVENNA

BUNNY EAR CACTUS

From the cactus family, this succulent is very common and multiplies easily.
Be careful with the thorns that irritate the skin with just one touch.

NATURAL HABITAT MEXICO
LIGHTING FULL SUN
SCIENTIFIC NAME OPUNTIA MICRODASYS

PEANUT CACTUS

The peanut cactus is one of the easiest to care for. Due to its natural habitat, it adapts well to warm climates.

NATURAL HABITAT ARGENTINA
LIGHTING FULL SUN
SCIENTIFIC NAME ECHINOPSIS CHAMAECEREUS

ENCYCLOPEDIA OF SUCCULENTS

Even succulent collectors have difficulty identifying species and it is almost impossible to know the names of them all. There are countless families, species and crossing of succulents, making the job of identifying them very difficult.

Don't know the name? At least know the family, easily recognised by its characteristics (shapes and colour), this way it will be simpler to know its origin and what care is needed.

PESTS, BEGONE!

CHAPTER 18
PESTS, BEGONE!

These are, without a doubt, your garden's biggest enemies.

APHID

CATERPILLARS

SLUGS AND SNAILS

ANTS

COCHINEAL

APHID

FUNGI

MITE

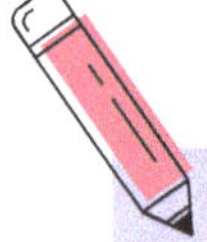

DO YOU RECOGNISE ANY OF THEM? WHAT IS YOUR SOLUTION FOR FUNGI AND PESTS?

There's no way around it. Everyone who has plants at home or works with them will one day come across small pests in the garden.

Aphids, mites, slugs, snails, caterpillars, insects, ants and fungi seem to be united in the destruction of that plant that you love so much.

In this chapter, apart from teaching you how to get rid of them, I want to show you another view on fungi and pests: they are not the problem — just **one of the symptoms** of the disease.

It's very simple. Cochineals, for example, appear and multiply in weak plants with calcium deficiency. Aphids love plants with excess nitrogen, from over-fertilisation.

Fungi, in turn, are already present in nature and some are necessary for the maintenance of the ecosystem. However, when they encounter a very dry environment, shade or even a lot of humidity, they multiply quickly, compromising the health of the plant.

It is not difficult to imagine, from this, that the best way to combat fungi and pests is to treat the disease in your plants. There is no point in applying chemical pesticides without treating the cause, as the pests will return, even more resistant.

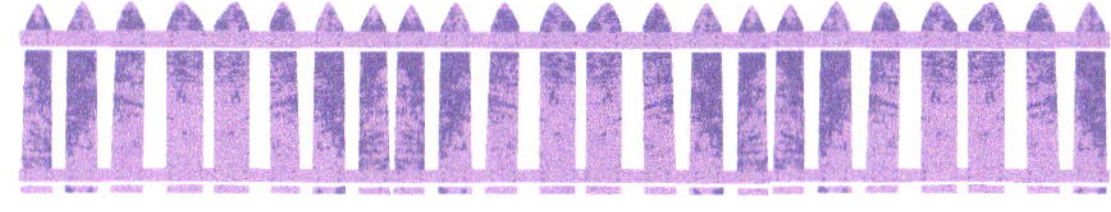

MAIN CAUSES

DRY WEATHER

HIGH AIR HUMIDITY

LACK OF FERTILISER

LACK OF LIGHTING

INSECT EGGS

MISUSE OF PESTICIDES

EXCESS WATERING

PROXIMITY TO OTHER DISEASED PLANTS

STEP-BY-STEP GUIDE TO COMBATING PESTS AND FUNGI

1º IDENTIFY THE DISEASE

Whenever you take care of your garden, take a quick look at your plants, look for insects, spots- or dropping of new leaves, or other abnormal signs. If you identify something unusual, find out what is causing the problem.

2º CLEANING

Give the sick plant a good cleaning. If it is small, it's ideal to wash the entire plant, delicately, with water and neutral detergent, eliminating all insects and eggs. Soak the entire vase in this solution for 2 hours, if possible.

For large vegetation, a hose bath or strong jet of water and pruning the diseased parts is enough.

3º TREATMENT

Now that the insects are gone, it's time to treat the cause of their appearance. Inadequate lighting? Did you water too much? Lack of fertiliser? If possible, isolate the sick plant from the others and adjust its care. For example, if your plant has fungus due to excessive watering and shade, reduce the frequency of watering and bring it closer to natural light.

4º APPLICATION OF NATURAL PESTICIDES AND FUNGICIDES

You already know that you shouldn't use any harmful chemicals in your garden. For the same reason that organic fertiliser is more recommended, the use of pesticides is even more harmful to your health.

This is the time when you should apply pesticides or fungicides to your sick plants, but try to opt for natural recipes, which you can make yourself at home. For organic recipes, spray the solution every night for at least 15 days. The idea is to use pesticides that would naturally repel these pests, out in the nature.

5º PAY ATTENTION

If you have followed all the previous steps, your garden should now be protected against your attackers. At this time, it is essential to pay attention to the slightest signs of a new attack or if your plant continues to be sick. If everything is OK, you will notice that new healthy leaves will appear and it will develop normally again.

ORGANIC RECIPES

ONION SAUCE

IDEAL AGAINST PESTS AND SMALL INSECTS.

- 1 whole onion
- 1 head of garlic
- Black pepper

Blend everything in a blender or mixer, with minimal water, just to make it easier to grind.

After that, pass it through a sieve until you obtain a liquid syrup from the mixture.

To dilute, for every 100ml of syrup add 1 litre of water.

Leave it to concentrate for a few hours and it is ready to be sprayed on your plants.

CINAMMON SAUCE

IDEAL AGAINST FUNGI.

- 10g horsetail (dried or fresh)
- 10g cinnamon powder
- 10g chamomile (dry or fresh)

Add approximately 500ml of water and make tea with all the ingredients.

After that, pass it through a sieve until you obtain a liquid syrup from the mixture.

To dilute, for every 100ml of syrup add 1 litre of water.

Let it cool and it is ready to be sprayed on your plants.

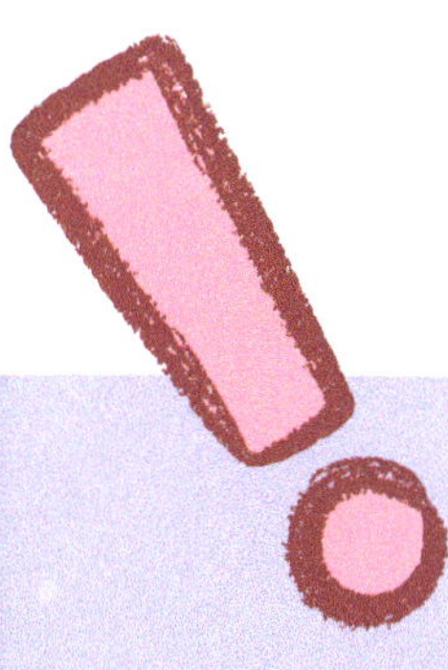

GOLDEN TIP

For other larger pests, the best way is manual cleaning. Make bait with sweet foods (papaya peel, melon) to attract slugs and snails and remove them from your garden.

VASES

CHAPTER 19

VASES

It is with great pleasure I say that you are a . So far, I have taught you basic knowledge to take care of your garden, keeping it healthy and developing. Watering, lighting, fertilisation, disease control. Garden maintenance is up to date.

How about we talk a little about decoration? After all, for indoor gardeners, with their evergrowing urban jungles, the appearance of the home is all about harmony and well-being. But anyone who believes that the choice of vases, only concerns decoration, is mistaken. Using the correct pot for each type of vegetation helps a lot in caring for your plants.

PLASTIC

Plastic pots are, without a doubt, the cheapest. Some may not be as decorative, but they have a characteristic that, if used correctly, can make watering in the garden easier: they **keep the substrate moist**, as the excess water is only released through the holes in the bottom.

For tropical plants and others that require daily watering, plastic pots are a good option.

CERAMIC

Unlike plastic pots, ceramic pots are recommended for plants that are more sensitive to watering, such as succulents, for example.

This material **absorbs excess water**, keeping the substrate's humidity controlled and protecting the plant's roots.

Nothing stops you from painting them to match your decor.

CEMENT

Cement pots have a similar function to ceramic pots, as they are capable of absorbing moisture.

Furthermore, they are easily found in **different sizes and shapes**. Painted or in the natural colour of the cement. You can even be adventurous and make them at home. For these reasons, it is a favourite among succulent collectors.

GLASS

Glass vases are certainly the most elegant and are perfect for interior decoration and terrariums.

However, as a gardener, I have to tell you that it is the quickest way to kill your plants. As it is not possible to make holes in this material, **excess water will accumulate** in the roots of your plant.

If you opt for this type of pot, choose plants grown in water or that are very resistant.

WOOD

Wood is another material suitable only for supports or cachepots.

Over time and watering, **wood will rot and grow fungus**, no matter how varnished it is. Always place another vase inside to conserve the material.

ALUMINUM

This type of pot retains moisture in the substrate, just like plastic pots. The difference is its **strength and durability**.

Most of these pots are sold as supports (without holes). But if you want to grow your plants directly in them, you can easily make your own holes with a drill.

IS GARDENING

FOR ME?

CHAPTER 20
IS GARDENING FOR ME?

To the indoor gardeners who made it to the end of this book, my heartfelt congratulations. I hope you discover how much gardening increases life quality and that you cultivate the garden of your dreams.

Let's take a final test? At the end of it, I'm sure you'll see how much you've learned and understand that you're ready to enter the world of gardening with success!

At the end of this chapter you will also find an empty maintenance calendar for you to fill out and use for your own garden.

DO YOU HAVE GREEN FINGERS?

1 HOW DO YOU FEED YOUR PLANTS?

A With industrial fertiliser.

B I buy or make my organic fertiliser at home.

C Do I have to feed them?

D I don't need it, they have everything they need in the ground.

2 HOW DO YOU DEAL WITH PESTS?

A I throw the plant away.

B I apply chemical pesticides or poison.

C I don't care, I leave them there.

D I have several natural pesticide recipes ready for every situation.

3 IF I SEE APHIDS IN THE GARDEN...

A I wash my plant and apply pesticide.

B I wait, because they will go away on their own.

C They are a sign that everything is okay.

D There is no treatment, I have to throw everything away.

4 WHEN SHOULD I REPOT MY PLANT?

A Never.

B Once every three months.

C Once a year.

D When the pot is too small for the final size of the plant.

5 WHAT IS ETIOLATION?

A The name of an organic fertiliser.

B What happens when I water too much.

C Normal plant growth.

D Abnormal plant growth due to inadequate lighting.

6 HOW TO USE MANURE IN THE GARDEN?

A Mix it into the substrate.

B Manure is not used in gardening.

C Mix it in water and spray it on the plants.

D It is a great pesticide against bugs.

7 WHAT ARE THE IDEAL SOIL LAYERS?

A Drainage and substrate.

B Substrate and vegetation cover.

C Drainage, substrate and vegetation cover.

D There is no right soil layer.

8 WHICH OF THESE TOLERATES SHADE?

A Fruit tree.

B Plants of tropical origin.

C Flowers in general.

D Plants originating from the savannah.

9 WHAT REQUIRES MORE WATERING?

A Vegetables in general.

B Succulents.

C Succulents in general, with the exception of cacti.

D Temperate climate plants.

10 WHY DOESN'T YOUR PLANT BLOOM?

A It is normal for some plants not to flower.

B Excessive watering.

C Lack of fertiliser and light.

D Because it's a succulent and they don't flower.

If you answered 4 or more questions correctly, gardening is already part of your life.
Always keep learning and improving your gardening skills. Your garden will thank you!

✔ **1** - B; **2** - D; **3** - A; **4** - D; **5** - D; **6** - A; **7** - C; **8** - B; **9** - A; **10** - C.

MAINTENANCE CALENDAR

Here is an example of how you can set up your maintenance calendar to keep your garden healthy. **Do not follow this calendar**, it wasn't made for your garden or based on your needs.

GARDEN MAINTENANCE CALENDAR - EXAMPLE | BY GABRIELA VILHELMSSON

TYPE	PLANT	BLOSSOM	FERTILIZING	PRUNING	WATER	POT	PREVENTION OF DISEASE AND PESTS
SHADE LEAVES	Monstera deliciosa		**September** - Complete fertilization (humus, manure) **November** - between fertilization - humus, bark **April** - calcium, phosphorus, potassium, sulfur – humus	**Always** - Pruning cleaning, dry, old leaves.	Every 2 days Spray with water 2x a day in dry weather	Placing a tutor for fixation	**November** - Fungicide **April** - Fungicide
SHADE LEAVES	Devil's Ivy Plant		**September** - Complete fertilization (humus, manure) **November** - between fertilization - humus, bark **April** - calcium, phosphorus, potassium, sulfur – humus	**Always** - Pruning cleaning, dry, old leaves. **Every 40 days** - Size maintenance pruning.	Daily OR Water twice a day in dry weather		**November** - Fungicide **April** - Pesticide
SHADE LEAVES	Anthurium	**ALL YEAR** (if abundant light)	**September** - Complete fertilization (humus, manure) **November** - between fertilization - humus, bark **April** - calcium, phosphorus, potassium, sulfur – humus	**After flowering** - complete pruning, old and yellowed leaves.	Every 2 days	Repotting in a bigger vase	**November** - Fungicide **April** - Pesticide
FLOWER	Orange Lily	**SPRING / SUMMER**	**After flowering** - Complete fertilization (humus, manure) **September** - between fertilizations - humus, bark	**After flowering** - complete pruning, replanting the bulb.	Every 2 days	Bulb repotting after flowering	**November** - Fungicide **April** - Pesticide
CACTUS	Cactus Opuntia Microdasys	**1x YEAR**	**September** - Complete fertilization (bokashi or similar) **April** - calcium, phosphorus, potassium, sulfur – bark		1x week	Repotting in a ceramic vase	**November** - Fungicide **June** - Pesticide **February** - Pesticide

It's time to put everything you've learned into practice and create your own maintenance calendar! Fill in according to where you live. Remember the importance of knowing your environment before creating your garden. What is your biome? ___________________

GARDEN MAINTENANCE CALENDAR

TYPE	VEGETATION	BLOSSOMING	FERTILISING	PRUNING	IRRIGATION	REPPOTING	PREVENTION OF PESTS AND DISEASES	OTHER

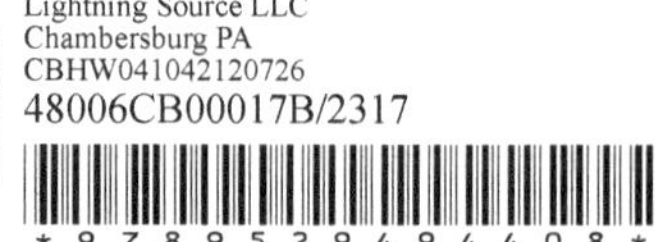
9 789529 494408